Essential Song

Indigenous Studies Series

The Indigenous Studies Series builds on the successes of the past and is inspired by recent critical conversations about Indigenous epistemological frameworks. Recognizing the need to encourage burgeoning scholarship, the series welcomes manuscripts drawing upon Indigenous intellectual traditions and philosophies, particularly in discussions situated within the Humanities.

Essential Song

Three Decades of
Northern Cree Music

Lynn Whidden

**WILFRID LAURIER
UNIVERSITY PRESS**
www.wlupress.wlu.ca

LAURIER

Inspiring Lives.

This book has been published with the help of a grant from the Canadian Federation for the Humanities and Social Sciences, through the Aid to Scholarly Publications Programme, using funds provided by the Social Sciences and Humanities Research Council of Canada. Wilfrid Laurier University Press acknowledges the support of the Canada Council for the Arts for our publishing program. We acknowledge the financial support of the Government of Canada through the Book Publishing Industry Development Program for our publishing activities. This work was supported by the Research Support Fund.

Canada

Canada Council Conseil des arts
for the Arts   du Canada

ONTARIO ARTS COUNCIL
CONSEIL DES ARTS DE L'ONTARIO
an Ontario government agency
un organisme du gouvernement de l'Ontario

Library and Archives Canada Cataloguing in Publication

Whidden, Lynn, 1946–
    Essential Song : three decades of northern Cree music / Lynn Whidden

(Indigenous studies series)
Includes bibliographical references and index.
Issued in print and electronic formats.
ISBN 978-1-55458-613-4 (paperback).—ISBN 978-1-55458-144-3 (pdf)—
ISBN 978-1-55458-819-0 (epub)

    1. Cree Indians—Québec (Province)—Music—History and criticism. 2. Cree Indians—Manitoba—Music—History and criticism. I. Title. II. Series: Indigenous studies series (Waterloo, Ont.)

ML3563.9.W572 2007   781.62973071   C2007-901535-2

Cover design by Gary Blakeley. Text design by Catharine Bonas-Taylor.

First paperback printing 2017

© 2007 Lynn Whidden

Published by Wilfrid Laurier University Press
Waterloo, Ontario, Canada
www.wlupress.wlu.ca

Contents

iv *Contents*

Personal Elements in Song Content 63
The Words • Trout Song
Song Presentation 67
Presentation • Rhythmic Elements • Form • Melodic Elements
The Cree Sound Ideal 73

4 Hymns and Hunting Songs 75
Missionaries and Cree Song 76
Adapting Hymns to Suit Tradition 84
Gospel Music 87
Amazing Grace

5 Country Music: How Can You Dance to Beethoven? 91
Cree Contributions to Country Music 97

6 Powwow in the Subarctic 101
Round Dances 109
Powwow Song Characteristics

7 The Powwow: From the South to the Subarctic 113
The Way He Walked Was Different 115
Powwow: The Popular Music for the Native American 119

Conclusion 121

Afterword by Stan Louttit 127

Appendix I 129
Frequently Sung Hymns in Chisasibi, Quebec 129

Appendix II 132
The Eighty-Six Songs, with Topics and Commentary,
of the 1982 and 1984 Collections 132

Notes 153

List of Sources 157

Bibliography 163

Index 171

CD Track Listing 176

Table of Figures

Foreword

As a valuable resource of musical heritage for the Cree Nation, this book offers an opportunity for all readers to gain an awareness of the struggle, strength, and wisdom of Indigenous people. It also supports the need to include, respect, and preserve Indigenous cultures as an integral part of human heritage and the cultural landscape of this country.

The loss of oral traditions has proven to be greater with increasing advancements in technology over the past century. However, with the new technologies and tools readily accessible to our youth, future generations may be able to record and retell our fragile traditions and preserve our endangered culture.

Essential Song presents a culturally significant outline of the musical history of my people known as Northern Cree First Nations. Lynn Whidden traces the unique and poignant story of traditional Cree songs, within the context of their history and natural environment, through their evolution and abandonment due to the impact and imposition of western values, culture, religion, and music.

Eric Robinson

Eric Robinson, born in Norway House Cree Nation and a member of the Cross Lake Cree Nation and Treaty #5, currently serves as Minister of Aboriginal and Northern affairs for the Province of Manitoba. Eric's vision, strength, and tireless commitment to improving the lives and opportunities of his people are based on his continued practice of traditional values, language, and ceremonies. Part of his continuing role as traditional teacher and leader includes facilitating ceremonies and celebrations as well as serving as a master of ceremonies for powwows. His first introduction to the author occurred through a music class taught by Lynn Whidden while he attended Inter-Universities North in 1979.

Acknowledgements

This book owes its existence to the Cree people to whom music means so much: the Cree hunters and their wives; my students from whom I continue to learn; and all the contemporary musicians who seek not just to be entertained, but to make life meaningful with music. I am particularly grateful for the work of three Cree interpreters—Elizabeth Kitty and Violet Bates of Chisasibi, Quebec, and Edna Voyageur of Misstassini, in northern Quebec—and for the able translations of Stella Bearskin and Matthew Rat, of Chisasibi. My gratitude goes also to the young people I talked to in the 1970s about identity and the powwow who continue their search for a rightful place for indigenous people in Canadian society and remain willing to talk with all those truly interested. Ed Azure was outstanding in his efforts to help me understand the problems and potential of his people. You can read in some detail here about his dedication to teach others through the oral narratives. I have tried to show their devotion to, and affinity for, the realm of sound. To the Cree, music is an imperative, and hence the book's title, *Essential Song*.

Most authors set out to write a book, but in my case I realized that after several decades of intense interest in the songs of Canada's subarctic Cree, I *had* a book. After talking with people, recording songs and sounds, and reading all the relevant articles and books I could find, I had many files of notes—and many more not-so-filed notes too. Such an unplanned procedure does not make for the easy assembly of information, and this book would never have happened without the encouragement of Robert Brockway and Catherine Brockway, and especially the hands-on help of Katie, who became my patient copy-editor. Many others have lent scholarly and technical support. David Westfall contributed to my knowledge of Woods Cree, Brian Craik to my knowledge of Eastern Cree, and Larry Fisher to my understanding of northern music history.

And finally, thanks goes to Richard and Rachel, who were with me all the way.

Prologue: The Cree Come to Campus

To my students

The Early Years—1970s and 80s

In the 1970s and 1980s, there was one thing that I could be certain of on the first day with a new class of northern Native students: no one would interrupt my lecture. I had taught Native student teachers from remote areas for over twenty years, and, while I noticed small changes over this time in the people's demeanor and their knowledge about the rest of the world, I marvelled at the stability of the Cree personality. And I stress *marvelled* because their approach did not fit the "on time, bottom line" system of the western world, and this caused them no end of trouble as they trained to be teachers.

Non-Natives have set out to make Aboriginals into westerners since their first encounters. Contact history shows wars, missionary work, bureaucracy, and residential schools designed for assimilation. Indian leaders complied with, and supported, some of these attempts; they were particularly approving of education. Another slimmer chapter of this history is unfolding with the teacher education projects begun in the 1970s by several Canadian universities. The projects have names such as "Project for the Education of Native Students" (PENT) and "Brandon University Northern Teacher Education Program" (BUNTEP). These "access" projects have lower university entry requirements but intend, through supplements to the regular programmes of studies, to have equivalent exit standards. Many elementary school teachers have graduated from these projects, and now teach in Native communities across Canada.

It is interesting to note that the Native presence changes the content and structure of the university programs, despite the efforts of educators to keep the courses and course content "by the book." Each class of Native graduates changes the system and the approach of the teachers, bringing to mind Robert Pirsig's observation in his book *Lila* that it is the

Aboriginal population that has made North America quite different from Europe:

> The slips went on and on detailing European and Indian cultural differences and their effects, and as the slips had grown in number a secondary, corollary thesis had emerged: that this process of diffusion and assimilation of Indian values is not over. It's still with us, and accounts for much of the restlessness and dissatisfaction found in America today. Within each American these conflicting sets of values still clash. (1991, 46)

Unfortunately, the Native personality has been a poor fit with an institution where performance is assessed largely by ability to meet deadlines. Our systems are unforgiving when it comes to meeting individual needs and personal upsets: while this may be a hurdle to the non-Native, it has often been a complete block to Native students who may opt to quit a situation so alien to their inclination. The aforementioned access programs do operate in a more flexible way within the university structure, but, even so, interacting with the university bureaucracy is often difficult and dependent on individual compromise.

Overall, non-Native institutions, designed to deal with large numbers of people, have a structure that has been inimical to the Aboriginal. For example, I have had Native students successfully complete all but the last week of a course, and then disappear without explanation. No number of practical considerations, such as the time and money invested, or their future career, convinced them to finish. Naturally curious about this behaviour, I discovered a group of students who did not compartmentalize their emotional lives: a personal problem could diffuse through all aspects of their lives and immobilize them until it was resolved. They reacted in entirety, and did not show a "stiff upper lip."

They did the task when the time and the feeling were right, and they did it well, without rushing. For example, no matter my resolve, my classes did not begin at the specified time; they began when everyone had arrived. Wise educators in those days soon learned to ignore the clock and use the beginning of lessons for joking and informal education. ("Coffee breaks" repeated this pattern on a smaller scale.) The behaviour brings to mind Philips' observation:

> If it is possible to speak in terms of choices having been made without the implication of an active collective conscious making the choices, then it would be appropriate to suggest, as I have already in greater detail elsewhere (Philips 1972), that the Warm Springs Indians repeatedly made organizational choices that maximize the possibility that everyone who

wants to participate is given the chance when he or she chooses to and in the way he or she chooses to. (1974, 107)

The instructor had more control over classroom space, yet Native mothers must be the originators of on-site child care. Many of my classes had at least one child clinging to a mother or young grandmother. Often a different child did this every day, so there was clearly behind-the-scenes coordination. These children were invariably quiet and undemanding of their caregiver. They did not need to be entertained, and spent much of their time watching, listening, and apparently creating. One time, at the end of a day observing my music class, a three-year-old Inuit child knew very well how to set up the xylophone, putting the bars in the correct slots. When he took one apart, and I suggested he put it together again, he said, "No—racetrack," and proceeded to put the bars on sideways so that he could run his toy car along them!

Individuals had no desire to stand out from the class, and it was rare to see a hierarchy develop. There was palpable disapproval for individual grandstanders and there were few answers proffered or questions asked. When they spoke to each other or the instructor, their voices were quiet. Their clothing reflected the desire for conformity—it was informal and tended towards subdued, dark colours. It was not unusual for many to wear their coats throughout class, in a room which many would consider overheated. There was no hustle and bustle at entry and leave-taking. In fact, economy of effort was very much a part of the students' way of presenting themselves. Like their children, the students watched and listened. They offered little facial expression or body language to indicate they were engaged, except for jokes, in which they participated wholeheartedly.

English was a second language for many Native students. This, and the cultural differences in communication cues, challenged me to modify my teaching techniques. For example, I tended to use different vocabulary and sentence structure, and repeat ideas more than usual. Questions were built into course outlines to encourage students to think uniformly about the materials they were required to read. Some non-Native teachers overcompensated for cultural differences with an unusually vivacious and/or aggressive teaching style which did appear to engage minds and hearts, temporarily at least, but I have often wished that I could ask the recipients of this sometimes outlandish behaviour what they thought! All in all, non-Native teachers have been perplexed by the lack of feedback from students, which makes it difficult to fine-tune their teaching.

I sometimes think there was no harder job than teaching western music to Native students in the "teacher access" programs begun in the 1970s.

About two-thirds of the student teachers were women. This resulted in unusually silent music classes, for women were shy before non-family members. This was evident to me early in my career when I recorded songs in their communities. While the men would decide upon a song, describe it to me, and then sing it, the women would make many nervous attempts and often the song would dissolve into giggles. For example, one hunter had to urge his wife, Mary, to sing her songs for me, and she finally did so nervously, in a high clear voice.

Women sang constantly to their infants as they worked, but they worked alone and sang only for themselves and their families. Hence, evaluation in a university music course had to be structured differently from the usual public display of skills such as singing a melody, or clapping a rhythm. I had to plan music activities as group work, and evaluate students privately or with group listening rather than individual performance tests.

Moreover, our concept of music evaluation was foreign to Native students with whom I worked. The hunters stressed the importance of getting the words right. It was a way to get the job done, and in the case of the hunters, absolutely essential for a successful hunt. The value of a song was in its correct use, not in an ability to manipulate certain elements of the song. As I shall show, this holistic acceptance of music applies to contemporary music wherein the emotional response evoked is valued more highly than the technical skills of the musicians.

For the non-Native, evaluation and analysis of music go hand in hand. But for the Native people I encountered in the 1970s, music, like all phenomena of nature, made sense only in its context; it was not considered an object which can be pulled apart for study. Instead, music was a living process with great power, and the analysis of music into durational, melodic, and other structural elements for study caused problems for the students. Furthermore, written music, while acknowledged as a useful memory aid, had no roots in a culture that was transmitted orally. It was extremely difficult for adult students, many of whom played music by ear, to learn music notation.

Administrators asked me to train choirs to sing in harmony and to develop high-voiced singing, telling me, "It's been done before." But the Cree had no tradition of blended part-singing upon which to build and, in the North, the outer limits of vocal ranges, such as soprano and bass, were rarely used or heard in the 1970s and 80s. Music lessons teaching these techniques were not often available (and still are not), partly due to lack of funding but also, I suspect, due to a lack of interest.

On the last day of a music course, it was not uncommon for students to leave behind their books, notes, and even instruments. Many teachers saw this as evidence that the course had little meaning for them, but another interpretation is that the students were living in the present: they had no desire to collect and store items that had no immediate use. The Native lack of acquisitiveness extended to learning itself. Few students were greedy to learn more than necessary, to acquire knowledge for knowledge's sake. They did not display an active, aggressive approach to learning, and never asked direct, hard-hitting questions. They learned what was required (again, economy of effort). Nor, in my early teaching days, was there a desire for higher grades, although this is fast changing now that student funding may be related to grades.

Despite the educator's attempts to offer a course that fitted both Native predilections and university requirements, one suspected that the students were merely going along with demands, and that the music taught had little relevance to their lives. Instead, students loved the music their people had made their own over the generations. Many of them played by ear on portable instruments such as fiddles or guitars. In fact, most male students did play or at least had tried to play these instruments.

Even the introduction of indigenous music to make the curricula more relevant did not ring true in the classroom. Traditional song in a classroom was so far removed from its original function that it had little meaning and gave scant satisfaction; it lived only when it fulfilled the somatic mood for which it was intended. To them, it was no longer a living, meaningful message, and certainly not a powerful medium used to hunt and to heal. My students saw the scholarly study of their own traditions as a white pursuit. As late as 1998, one wrote the following:

> The music and the dance deserve a study because many white people would want to find out about the music and dance in the community and how it started back then. These whites would want to know what kind of music is played in the ceremonies that occur in Hollow Water, and how the drum and the rattles sound while singing with the instruments. (Ashley Bushie, Hollow Water, Manitoba, 1998)

The Last Decade—the 1990s

By the 1990s, the northern students had changed in ways that now appear to be lasting. I could be interrupted by an outspoken question or comment. Native students, women noticeably so, spoke with assurance before the entire class, and in standard English. Students wore brighter clothing and more adornments. Classes began more or less on time, with noisier discussion and more energetic exchange. Now there was a choir that sang louder, and with enthusiasm for this form of expression.

Many students were now consciously proud of their heritage too, and took an active interest in researching their traditions. One student wrote: "There were no signs of Native culture, dance, or music in my home. The closest I ever came to my Native culture was seeing my dad wear moccasins. Yes, I did speak Cree fluently and I knew I was Native, but I had nothing else to associate my Indian identity with" (Belinda Clark, Lynn Lake, MB, September 2000). They wanted to know their history, and to understand modern events such as the powwow, an innovation in northern life. Many of the students spoke Cree and Ojibwe, and were proud of it, but unhappy that they might be the last generation to speak the Algonquian language fluently. I present the story of Cree song here, in the hope that young people will recognize that they have a music heritage, that they will cherish their song tradition, and that they will build upon it to create songs for the youth of the twenty-first century.

Introduction

As the title *Essential Song* suggests, in this book I strive to show the fundamental place of song in subarctic hunting life. The northern Cree exemplify the human need for song, which I define here as an oral expression carried primarily in the singer's mind. Such songs are often learned from an ancestor and are an organic part of the singer's environment. As you will read, the Cree, throughout a time of enormous social change, maintained song as an oral, local, and spiritual tradition.

This book records observations, over thirty years (1970–2000), of subarctic Cree song in the Canadian provinces of Manitoba and Quebec. The context and function of songs and song-making are emphasized as much as the music, in emulation of the Cree approach to song. The text accompanies some of my audio recordings of hunting songs sung by six Cree men in the early 1980s.[1] Apart from the analysis of the hunting songs, I include a history of Cree oral forms and some discussion of recent transformations of Cree music.

The hunting songs you hear on the accompanying recording grew out of the sounds of the subarctic. For all but two or three months of the year, the air temperature is below freezing. The fragrant spruce forests and animals are silent under a blanket of snow, broken only by the occasional raucous call of a raven. Spring, in contrast, brings an outpouring of sound. Snow melts into roaring rapids, geese call overhead as they fly north for the summer, and awakening animals join the chorus. The Cree living around James Bay hear the sea ice begin to groan as it breaks up. In fall, they hear the continual rainfall as eastern winds pick up moisture from the bay and drop it on the coast.

A few of the Cree songs I recorded in the Chisasibi area focused on the terrain and weather, seeking such things as a change in the wind direction, but it is the animals—mammals, birds, and fish—which the Cree hunters favoured as song topics. The basin of La Grande River offered a wide variety of animals for them to sing about because this region is a transition zone between the middle and high subarctic. Southern fauna live alongside northern species such as the Arctic fox.

Because of the diversified habitats, the soundscape is alive with wildfowl and river birds. Six of the eighty-six songs I recorded were about Canada geese, an important source of food for the Cree. Other songs were about the loon, the partridge, the snowbird, and the migrating brant geese. The hunters also sang about fish—local species include whitefish, cisco, longnose suckers, pike, walleye, white suckers, rounds, burbot, and speckled trout (Berkes 1983, 5)—and the commonly hunted animal species, such as beaver, muskrat, lynx, otter, red fox, black bear, mink, rabbit, red squirrel, and martin. I recorded eight fox songs, five beaver, four otter, two porcupine, one muskrat, one hare, one deer, one lynx, and one whale. The white fox seemed to be of particular interest to the Cree, perhaps because of its scarcity in the Chisasibi area. Beaver was important for the Cree economy, reflected in the number of beaver-related songs and stories.

Not only did the Cree hunters know all the sounds the animals make, but also the appropriate sounds a hunter must make to attract them. Several hunters showed how fox and muskrat are attracted by the hunter's imitation of mouse sounds (a kissing sound made with the lips), while geese responded to imitation goose calls. A beaver was called by a sound that mimicked the noise of another beaver eating branches.

The James Bay Cree based their subsistence economy on these species. When I was recording these songs, hunting game still determined the lives of at least half the male population of Chisasibi, although it no longer dictated their dwelling place—only a few families chose to live year-round in a bush camp. Most now maintained a permanent dwelling in the town, and lived only temporarily in camps established for hunting.

The performance of the traditional hunting songs is linked to the continuance of subsistence hunting. Although there are exceptions, even the newest generation of Cree appear to value and enjoy bush food. The elders view it not only as physically and mentally nourishing but also as a medicine. Many old people are reluctant to eat most store-bought foods, and when they must, they do not feel properly nourished. It is also interesting to note that, in speaking of bush food, the Cree people stress how it feels as well as how it tastes. Certainly, I observed the pleasure with which families received presents of bush foods.

On a day when there is no bush food available, a typical dinner might be pork chops, potatoes, and canned corn. At every meal there are cookies, pies, or pudding. These foods are increasing in popularity. One young man told me that his grandmother doesn't understand why he prefers "white" food, and why he does not eat fish all the time, so he occasionally eats fish just to appease her.

The continued preoccupation of the Cree with hunting would seem to bode well for the survival of their songs, for clearly the songs are tied to their lives as hunters. But this is not a certain guarantee because traditional song is being challenged by other factors, such as weakening intergenerational relationships and, more importantly, the music and entertainment of the mass media. In northern Manitoba, while there is much local music, the hunting songs have not been heard for several generations. In northern Quebec the tradition is extant but imperilled. In an oral culture, the music must be understood, enjoyed, and shared, or it will not be performed. It must fit the needs of individuals and populations, or it will die. But oral transmission is only the beginning of this story, because after contact with non-Natives, the Cree were subjected to a barrage of information acquired first from literacy and then from the mass media.

New modes of media transmission have been enthusiastically adopted by isolated northerners because they fit the Cree preference for oral communication. The reading and writing of music is rare; the use of media technology is pervasive. Remarkably, the people have been able to fashion much non-Native music to fit their Cree ethos. Too often portrayed as victims of the white man and his culture, the Cree have adapted favourite hymns to sound more like the old Cree melodies; fiddle tunes were played with the rhythm of hunting songs, and country song became an oral communal tradition.

Paradoxically, the adoption of powwow music during recent decades signals the weakening of enduring local traditions. This radically different sound is part of a conscious attempt to take part in a broader Native American heritage, even though powwow music has no roots in northern Cree culture. On the other hand, the revitalization achieved through the powwow has led many Cree back to the study and appreciation of their own hunting culture.

History shows us that the Cree have not altered the hunting songs to fit their new circumstances. So far, I have discovered few conscious attempts to create, for example, a hybrid song of traditional and new sounds. Institutional education now includes Cree culture, but so far schools have not produced graduates capable of creating songs rooted in Cree style and language. If educators do manage to perpetuate the oral narratives through the schools, it is certain that they will be different, most certainly in function, if not in form.

My fascination with Native life began in the 1970s, when I moved to a northern Manitoba mining community to teach school music. There, I watched many Cree succumb to alcohol. They still lived and thought as their ancestors did, but sadly, the knowledge was fragmented and increasingly irrelevant to the demands of twentieth-century life. The hunting songs that were created from their immediate relationship with the animals and the land were disappearing, but the stories of *wesagajak*, the trickster, lived on, although few of the younger generation were listening.

As a musician, I wanted to hear the songs of subsistence hunters, and in 1974 I was fortunate to be able to record the traditional songs of the Caribou Inuit in Arviat, Nunavut, then called Eskimo Point, Northwest Territories. While still shaken from the abrupt change in their physical location (the Canadian government in 1957 began to move the Inuit from inland camps to more easily accessible locations), the elders of Arviat wanted to tell the story of their former life as hunters.[2] The "warm" hours of January 1974 that I spent listening to their songs and stories were an inspiration to carry on. So, when I returned south to Cree territory, I documented what I found in Manitoba: country music, hymns, powwow, and, above all, rich memories of the past contexts for song. Then, in the 1980s, with support from the National Museum Urgent Ethnology Program, I was fortunate to be able to live with the Cree of northern Quebec, and to record eighty-six of their hunting songs. At this time, none of the elders I visited spoke English, and my understanding of the songs and their context was entirely through the able work of interpreters Elizabeth Kitty and Violet Bates of Chisasibi, and the subsequent dedicated translating of Edna Voyageur of Misstassini. In the transcriptions presented in this book, I represent the translator's pauses as line breaks with the result that the song and story words have the appearance of poetry on the page. In this approach I follow Dennis Tedlock (1972) because it does make the narratives more accessible than they would be prose form. Moreover, I have written a brief anecdote at the opening of each chapter to set the emotional tone, so important to musical understanding.

While I was recording in the James Bay area of Quebec, other ethnologists were working equally hard to preserve indigenous musical traditions: Beverley Diamond, Raymond Pelinski, and Nicole Beaudry in the Arctic, and Richard Preston and Michael Asch in the subarctic, to mention only a few. These collections are now an invaluable part of Aboriginal mental history, useful for all of humankind to understand our music heritage.

The Cree hunting songs show us a consciousness shaped by a natural world wherein all is considered related and alive—including the songs themselves. The people I interviewed felt that their songs had the potential to change the material world, and that they were essential for physical and mental health. The songs revealed a mode of knowing gained not only from the physical world but also from dreams and narratives, both song and story. Now Cree communities have the same music choices as populations around the world. While some retain interest in the old songs, others approach music as non-Natives do, speaking of artists, hit songs, marketing, and entertainment. The Cree with whom I spoke, however, believe, as did their ancestors, that the old songs are powerful and must be treated with respect.

This book is organized by song genres, with the post-contact genres presented in the order that they were received by the Cree. I begin with the hunting songs, which were surely sung before contact with Europeans and then co-existed with European hymns. Then I discuss Gospel songs, which largely supplanted both the hunting songs and the old hymns. Next I look at the ongoing stream of country tunes that are popular across Canada's North, and why they have such appeal for Algonquian speakers. And lastly I present a lengthy discussion of powwow music in northern Manitoba to show the role of music in creating identity.

There are many approaches necessary to explain the Cree music of the past three decades. First, I foreground Cree understanding of their music, and use their words to describe the songs. In their conversations with me, the elders, who fear the loss of Cree ways, deemed it important to remember not only their songs, stories, and hymns, but also to explain carefully their meaning. Their joyful hunting songs showed the ordered, vital connection between man and animal and all of nature—and depicted the Cree cosmos. Younger generations are interested in thinking about and discussing the role and the contents of country and powwow music. Several remarked to me that music has a special place in the lives of First Nations people.

Second, I include history and ethnography, both spoken and written, to help provide a context for the songs. Many of the original performance contexts have disappeared, such as the Goose Dance in northern Manitoba, but there are rich texts available, both in written ethnographies and in the memories of elders.

Third, with the aid of western techniques of music notation and analysis, we can better understand music change, as the Cree leave behind the old hunting songs and hymns for contemporary genres such as country and gospel. The analysis shows that the Cree apply their cultural prerogatives to the sound and performance environment of the music they accept.

To date, powwow music remains the exception, for I have heard little in northern Cree powwow music to distinguish it from Plains powwow, though they have adhered to their own smaller contexts for its performance.

Finally, the Cree hunters' songs require us to consider the indispensable role of actively doing song, of relating narratives, as opposed to listening passively to music created outside of the community. Our ancestors' lives, although limited, have much to teach us about an everyday life that was joyful and susceptible to ecstasy. If we are to realize our full human potential, we must seek a balance of mind and body, value and fact. In this twenty-first century, many are cognizant of the weaknesses of a materialist approach for satisfaction, of a way of life in which human beings are separated from their physical environment. Knowledge is all in this information age, and it is easily captured and transmitted by means of words or other symbols. There is another dimension available to humankind we now call "traditional ecological" knowledge, which comes from lived experience and is not formally taught. It is an awareness of human nature within nature, created over the millennia, which has made humans uniquely successful adaptors, an awareness we must strive to appreciate and cultivate.

Musical Profiles of the Contributors

In 1982, and when I returned again in 1984, the Cree hunters I interviewed were resident in Chisasibi, Quebec. A few were still hunting. They were bright, alert, and energetic, a testament to their healthy lifestyle. The interviews, all conducted in their homes, were a delight, for they enjoyed talking and especially joking with the translator and me, and they wanted to share their songs and stories with future generations.

While all were subarctic hunters, known as "coasters" (meaning the Cree who lived along and close to the east shores of the Hudson Bay), each had his own songs and singing style. Moreover, the quite different experiences in their interactions with the non-Native community are reflected in their songs. The six hunters whose songs I recorded were William Jack, George Pepabano, Robert Potts, Abraham Martinhunter, Samson Lameboy, and Joseph Rupert.

WILLIAM JACK

In 1982, William Jack was sharp-eyed, trim, and energetic. When I and the translator, Elizabeth Kitty, arrived at his house, he was listening to taped fiddle music. A variety of young people came and left, and William welcomed them all. When asked his age, he joked, "one hundred and nine."

Figure 1: William Jack

It turned out that he genuinely did not know, although he estimated it to be somewhere between seventy and seventy-three. It remained a joy for him to go hunting. Time passed too quickly for him. He used to be a guide for hunters from the south who carried tape recorders and wanted to hear his stories. William's wife, hard of hearing and somewhat crippled, had house-keepers to help her. Of the couple's six children, only two daughters survived, but several grandsons were living.

William said that, a long time ago, people always used to ask him to sing. "I guess they thought I was a good singer," he told me. And indeed, with unusual vocal flexibility for a strong bass, his voice was a pleasure to hear. His singing was always legato, flowing into spoken sections and back to melody. The melodies circled around one pitch, and were strongly triadic but ornamented with vibrato and unaccented ornaments. The pulse of the songs was steady, quick, and dense with many notes per pulse, reflecting the polysynthetic nature of the Algonquian language. I recorded three of his seven songs twice, first in 1982 and then again in 1984. Although the second recordings contained small changes in internal rhythm, they began on identical pitches to the versions recorded two years earlier.

William said he had a song for every activity. His Goose Song was sung because he was so happy after his marriage. He sang his Beaver Song before he started to hunt in the morning. The Winterbird inspired a song to encourage William to move with greater speed while wearing snowshoes. Some of his songs caused great laughter among us. (The Trout Song was short, "because the trout was small.")

William had considerable personal power and spoke of the power of his songs. He believed, however, that no one still living in his community could use the songs and the drum to influence the hunting and weather.

GEORGE PEPABANO

George, a tall, slender, clear-eyed man, was born in August, 1907. When I visited in June 1982, his wife was deceased and he was living with his daughter, helping to care for his two grandchildren. George had lived at Fort George, and then, after the relocation of 1980, he lived in Chisasibi. He had great knowledge of and concern for the Cree way of life, and particularly the Cree language. He lamented the fact that the young people didn't sing in the old way and didn't speak Cree. He admonished our translator for using English and French in her Cree, saying, "You should try to speak all Cree." He stated that now the kids are interested only in television and

Figure 2: George Pepabano

tape recorders. George knew many hunting songs but felt that young people were no longer able to sing them. They never came to him to learn. His great-grandfather used the bow and arrow, not guns, to hunt, and was skilful at making canoes out of birchbark.

His songs belonged to his father and uncle. He told me that, unlike the stories, which change with each retelling, the songs keep their main theme and character intact. His sixteen songs dealt with topics from the hunting culture and its changes. He was the only person I met who sang about the porcupine, and he also had songs about the otter, and about a beaver that appeared like a gift. When pressed by the translator to sing a song about a woman, he said he had never sung about a woman before, so he sang about a hunter who had two female deer beside him. He was also the only one to sing about the "shaking tent" (a ceremony performed by a shaman with an audience to help him "see," to give him knowledge), and like William Jack he sang about the white man, although George's song was a critique of the disruption of the beaver by the white man, perhaps in response to the flooding caused by the hydroelectric dam constructed on the La Grande River.

The steady pulse and repetition of short, clearly demarcated musical phrases made George's singing distinctive. Perhaps his vocal style was shaped by fiddle music, because he was known as a good step dancer and, with his light tenor voice, a good singer. His daughter said he attracted people to listen, just like a television!

ROBERT POTTS

When he was interviewed in June 1982, Robert Potts was grey-haired and had recently lost his vision due to illness. He had worked hard as a hunter to feed his family, and said his songs helped him to go on even when he was hungry and tired. Robert was a poet by nature and his sixteen songs evoke images of his life. He described the geese as a "black cloud" and he called his sister "dawn girl." His wife told me that she heard him sing when they lived in the bush. (Interestingly, she knew of no women who do "serious singing," only singing for their children.)

Although frail, Robert's voice was pleasant. His songs were interspersed with talk, and the talking and singing merged in pitch. His songs were chant-like with a strong rhythm, the pulses often grouped in pairs to form short musical phrases. Like the other singers, the songs centred on a focus tone, and were dense with notes.

Figure 3: Robert Potts

ABRAHAM MARTINHUNTER

Abraham Martinhunter was about seventy-nine when I interviewed him
in 1984. He had just returned home from visiting with other aged friends
in the shopping centre, and said he wanted to talk to me before his wife
Daisy got started. He switched off the colour television, which had been on
since I arrived, and began to marvel at the changes he had seen in his lifetime. Many of these changes he sang about. He said that his people used
to preserve their geese in wooden barrels and make their own fiddles. When
the white man came, everything changed. Many traditional practices ended,
and the drums disappeared, to be replaced by Christian ceremonies and
hymn-singing.

Of the nineteen songs he sang for me, only seven were about the animals. Nonetheless, they are marvellous examples of density of content. For
example, of the Fox Song, he said: "In the song I sang about the bait and
also about the measuring stick. I'm singing about the white fox. I used to
kill a lot. You don't see white foxes anymore, they're extinct. When I was
in the water, in a canoe, I used to sing this song. That was my favourite, to
be in water."

The other songs described local scenes and events, and reflected Abraham's varied work experiences. He had lived inland and knew many places

and people unfamiliar to our translator. In three different songs, he sang about the huge waves and the seasickness of people on the boats he observed while on night duty. (His task was to guide the sailboats carrying sugar and tea along the coast of James Bay.) He also met the Inuit, and his song says that they were savage and fierce but now behaved like white men. He sang about the rapids at Kaniapiskau. He also added his own song element to traditional stories such as the bird sounds ("baya, baya, baya") in the legend of Chipaye's back, and a song in the story of Iashow, in which the main character prepares to cause water to burn and fire to help him overcome his wicked stepfather.

Abraham had a strong, clear bass voice. His songs, less triadic than William Jack's, centred on one tone; each note contained a slight waver; the pulse was less regular; and the rhythms quite complex. Overall they were more chant-like than William's. He also sang several faithful renditions of the metrical Christian hymn tunes, which were in great contrast to his own songs.

He said that he began to sing when he got older, to express his feelings and to tell about his hunting experience. One night he dreamed about two foxes, one very dark and one very light. Then he went out to hunt and killed fifteen foxes. Abraham knew many of the old stories and believed in the powers Native people had in the past.

SAMSON LAMEBOY

In 1984, Samson Lameboy was grey-haired and elderly, but his voice remained strong. He admired his mother, who lived to be a hundred and was very wise. Samson had a profound knowledge of the hunting way of life, and was chosen to ask the blessing at the June 1984 walking-out ceremony to mark the first steps outdoors of the one-year-old children.

His songs focused on the hunt. He began by saying it was hard living off the land, so the people were always fit, mentally and physically. When the hunting was poor, the people starved. He joked that now "the store doesn't run away from you." His favourite song topic and favourite animal to hunt was the goose. He said the geese were easiest to hunt because they came to you, just like in a hide-and-seek game. Samson was the only hunter to sing a whole song about which the translator said, "There are words, but I can't get them."

Samson sang his eight songs and one hymn with great intensity. His voice was higher-pitched and the quality more focused than that of the other hunters. The short, distinct phrases centred on one pitch, a focus tone, and the tempos were quick and steady. Like the other singers, Samson's

rhythmic patterns were dense with notes of short duration. The affirma-
tive sound of his songs was reflected in the topics. Samson said they could
kill game with their powers. His song about the fox would bring it running to you. One song tells about women cutting wood so that the men
would be successful at hunting, and tells of the happiness of the women
when they found a stand of trees suitable for firewood.

Samson had no sad songs. In fact, he said people once did not mourn
for the dead the way they began to do after receiving the Bible. Instead, they
would put nets around the camp so the spirit wouldn't pass. They would
wait, and towards evening they would celebrate and shoot their guns.

JOSEPH RUPERT

Joseph Rupert's memorable "Trout Song" is one of only two songs in the
collection that have translatable words. His songs had melodic tunes and
a quick, steady pulse.

During our one brief meeting in 1984, Joseph sang six hunting songs.
They were about the geese, the trout, the fox, the muskrat, and about a
man walking with snowshoes, which truly has a walking rhythm. The two
hymns he sang contrasted with these, being slow and having a straight
vocal quality quite different from the vibrato used for his hunting songs.

Joseph said the drums were gone by the time his grandfather died. His
father had described to him the starvation experienced by the grandfather's generation—as Joseph remarked to me, "Old-age pensions weren't
introduced then." In another anecdote suggesting a supernatural event,
Joseph described how his father and grandfather had set out on an empty
stomach to hunt and had caught a caribou. When they looked at their
tracks, it appeared that the young boy with them (Joseph) had flown while
chasing the caribou, because there were no tracks in the snow.

1

Song and Ceremony

This study describes some of the contexts for the performance of the old Cree songs. Although I discuss two groups from two different provinces, Manitoba and Quebec, fundamental similarities of climate and geography permit discussion of the northern Cree as an aggregate. They share an ancestral home in the northern part of Canada known to geologists as the Precambrian Shield, which took shape after the retreat of the last glacier some ten thousand years ago. Archaeological evidence and local stories tell us that this has been Cree homeland for several thousand years. The coastal Cree live on the low, flat, muskeg-covered plains that border Hudson Bay. Farther inland, Cree live along the great rivers—La Grande in Quebec and the Nelson River in Manitoba—which flow into Hudson Bay. Many southerners view these fast-flowing rivers solely as a source of hydroelectric energy, but to the Cree they are talked about and experienced daily, a living heritage. The history of these rivers is ever-present, as the people recall their ancestors' descriptions of the Frenchmen singing on the way down the Nelson. For a written account of this, we must turn to the diary of a Scot, Archibald McDonald, describing the journey of Governor George Simpson's men on their journey from York Factory to Norway House:

> As we wafted along under easy sail ... the Highland bagpipes in the Governor's canoe, was echoed by the bugle in mine! Then these were laid aside, on nearer approach to port, to give free scope to the vocal organs of about eighteen Canadians [French] to chant one of those voyageur airs peculiar to them, and always so perfectly rendered. Our entry ... was certainly more imposing than anything hitherto seen in this part of the Indian country." (Nute 1955, 250)

The term "Cree" is probably an English shortening of a seventeenth-century word, *Kiristinon*, which the French used to refer to a widespread group of people who spoke a similar language. Before contact with Europeans, each group of Cree named themselves according to geographic and ecological criteria; after contact, they were often identified by the post where they

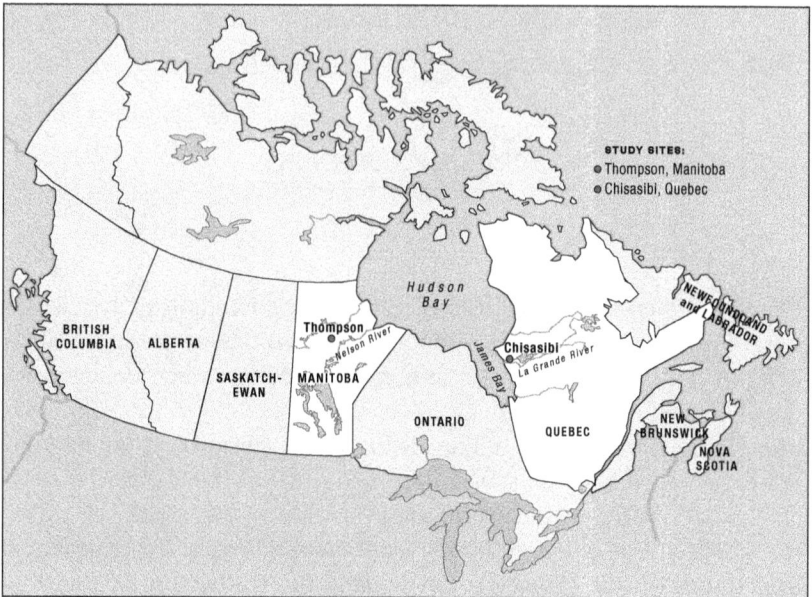

Figure 1.1: Map of Canada, with study sites indicated

traded. For example, the Albany River Indians called themselves *Kastechewan*, meaning "swift river." Some groups today are resuming their original names, such as the James Bay Cree at Chisasibi, who now prefer to be called *Iiyiyuu*.[1]

At time of contact in the seventeenth century, the Cree had a population of between fifteen thousand and twenty thousand. Today their numbers are four times greater: in the 1996 census, 76,475 persons were identified as Cree. Other groups in this area are the northern Ojibwa, Montagnais, Naskapi, and Algonquin, but the Cree are the largest and most widespread group in Canada. As one would expect, the details of Cree life across this vast northern region of Canada vary substantially. Even neighbouring communities use different Algonquian languages and have unique local histories about migrations, family groupings, and non-Native contacts.

The Cree homeland—the subarctic, which generally falls between latitudes 70° north and 90° north—is characterized by poor soil and extremes of climate. At Chisasibi, the average temperature is around 10°C during the warmest month, and for the coldest month it is less than –30°C. There are approximately eighty frost-free days each year, and 61 cm of precipitation. Thus the Cree have been a people who rely upon the hunt for their subsistence, seeking out all available resources: animals, birds, fish, and plants. Their traditional strategies for survival were mobility, food storage, and sharing. Nonetheless, elders recall periods of privation, even starvation. There are few species (but large numbers of each species) in the boreal forest, and populations of these are subject to cyclic fluctuations. For example, seasonal shortages occur particularly at the end of winter, just before the geese arrive, so these cyclical patterns of animal life need to be considered. In traditional Cree life, planning was crucial and the knowledge of experienced hunters was highly valued.

Skilled hunters, physically adept and knowledgeable about animal ways, have always been respected leaders. Animals, too, were respected as self-sacrificing, self-aware, immortal souls who gave themselves in return for proper thankfulness; if treated contemptuously, however, they would withhold themselves. For this reason, the bones of the bear would be placed on specially constructed platforms so that the dogs could not chew them. Moreover, if an animal offered itself by coming within the purview of the hunter, it had to be killed as a matter of obligation.

The animals used to be the foundation of Cree survival. In the past, hunters were inextricably linked to them with their songs. The songs contained facts about the appearance and behaviour of the ideal, healthy animal, and about local ecology. While rooted in the experience of generations, songs could also be changed to fit immediate needs. But, most importantly, they were vehicles for communicating with the spirit of the animals. They were prayers and predictions that helped to influence the outcome of the hunt.

Ecological uniformity across the north has resulted in a broad similarity of culture among Cree peoples, with common elements in stories and songs across the subarctic. For instance, the Cree distinguish between two kinds of narrative: the *aatiyookan* that tell of universal truths and give rules for proper living and for relating to other beings, and the *tipaachimoon* that tell of personal knowledge and everyday happenings. I would have liked to make more comparisons between the hunting songs, *nikamon*, of the coastal Cree of eastern James Bay and those of the Manitoba Cree, but, unfortunately, few such songs are now being sung in northern Manitoba. There *were* songs, as shown in Robert Brightman's ethnography of northern Manitoba Cree, *Grateful Prey* (2002). In this book, Brightman provides the words to several hunting songs sung in Pukatawagan in the 1980s. In other Manitoba communities, people recall hearing the old songs but cannot sing them. For example, one person described an old man singing with great emotion and beating upon a pie plate for rhythm because he lacked a drum. No one knew what he was singing, but they did know he was trying to find out or "see" something and was asking the Creator to help him. He sang his song three times; then finally began to "see," but in a way that only he could understand (Personal Communication, 1981).

The Drum and the Rattle

A common feature across the vast Cree lands was the drum, *taawahekan*. In 1981, elder Roddy Garrick in the northern village of Wabowden, Manitoba (previously a resident of Cross Lake), described seeing a drum made from caribou hide. The fur was removed and then stretched on a frame similar to the one used to prepare beaver pelts.[2] "A birch tree was bent and using sturgeon bladder, the hide was glued on, both top and bottom," he recalled. "Once it dried it was solid. Some of the drums had two strings inside, with a bunch of round small bones attached that made a noise when it was hit. They had a little hammer to hit it." Mr. Garrick said the drums were placed beside the fire and tested from time to time until the sound was right (Wolanski 1981). The East Cree drum of Mistassini, as described by Rogers (1967, 172), was similar to the Manitoba drum described above—it was a two-headed circular drum, made of a piece of larch five feet long and covered with caribou skin. The two hides were secured on either side of the cylindrical frame, with two hoops fastened by laces. A thread snare was stretched between the two outer hoops across the heads. From the thread hung four or five small pieces of wood, leg bones from fetal moose or caribou. Adrian Tanner (1979, 147) reported that these fetal bones were treated with respect, hung up on a wall or tent pole, and often used as buzzers on a drum. Rogers also noted a decoration of red dots around the circumference of the drumhead, with a cross and circle of red dots at the centre. Speck interpreted the red dots as shamanic symbols (1935, 173). More recently (1983), Edna Voyageur, an East Cree woman who grew up in Mistassini, Quebec, described the drums she grew up with as being approximately one and a half feet in diameter with a birchwood frame. The moose-hide head was sewn on with sinew. The drum was either held in one hand (with no handle) or suspended from the frame of the tent and struck with the other hand or with a beater. She said the drum itself made a soft sound, while a string of small bones across the top gave a rattling sound (1983).

Rogers (1967, 122) and Speck (1935, 175) give similar descriptions of the rattle (*she she gon*, in East Cree). Each writer describes a hoop constructed from birch or maple and covered with caribou- or moose-hide, sewn tightly along the midline of the hoop. Rogers reports that occasionally an entire fish skin was used, but this was considered less attractive than hide. Shot was put inside. A handle, an extension of the hoop, was decorated by carving and sometimes with red paint or ribbons. Other objects such as a small tin box containing shot might serve as a rattle.

In an 1823 letter to his father, fur-trade clerk George Nelson described his experiences with the Cree and Ojibwe of Lac la Ronge in northern Saskatchewan. Throughout the text, Nelson mentions the rattle, and provides two lengthy discussions of the drum. Both instruments were used to ensure a successful hunt. In one instance, nothing was caught with the first drumming, but with the second, a bear was captured, as the shaman had predicted.

In 1982, I interviewed Harry Hughboy of Wemindji, Quebec, and asked him to describe how the drums were used in ceremonies when he was growing up. Here is his recollection:

> The people that I remember from long ago used the drum a lot
> To sing, to express themselves
> When a certain individual was called upon to sing
> We would all gather in one tent
> People would sit in a circle
> And the individual would sit in a circle with the others
> The drum would be tied from the top of the tent
> Then he would start singing
> He would start singing about different happenings in his life—animals,
>   hunting
> He would make his songs up as he felt
> And at times when the hunt was very scarce
> And people were hungry
> There would be only small game to hunt, small birds
> And so the drum would be used to help the hunt
> And an old man would be called upon to use the drum and to sing
> And so he would sing about big game like beaver, deer
> That's how the hunt got better
> It seemed like when he was singing, he brought back the animals
> And at times when the hunt was very scarce
> The men would be hit the hardest
> Because they would have no energy
> It seemed like the women had more strength, willpower
> To overcome weakness from the lack of food
> And so the women would go out and hunt
> While the men recuperated.
>
> One time my father led me to a place
> Where it looked like there had been an old camp

That was the time when people really had hard times
When the hunt was scarce
One old man was called upon to cause the wind
To be from the southern direction
Because the south wind brings the geese
So they asked this old man if he could do everybody a favour
It was during those times when people didn't have English names
This old man's name was "Foxskin"
And so all the young men waited for this old man to start singing
And so they were going to call and cause the south wind to blow

The old man sang all night and he sang until morning
And then he went to wake up the young hunters and said,
"The south wind is blowing, get up and do your hunt,"
And so the young men prepared to do their hunting
And sure enough the birds came back.

The Indians of today are not like they used to be
Now they don't know how to drum and sing as they used to do.

[At this point, the translator added that it is a skill to learn, like other
    hunting skills]

By drumming the man would know where the game was
And then he would tell the young men
So he would tell the hunters to go to that particular place
And the hunters would go
It would be sometimes near a lake
Sure enough they would find game there like deer, caribou
So that's how good they were with the drum and singing
Through that they would know where the game was without seeing the
    game

The rattle and drum served similar functions and were played sepa-
rately or together. Sometimes the rattle served as a beater for the drum. The
rattle was used by the shaman to accompany his spiritual songs, and appears
to have been a necessary part of the Lac la Ronge "shaking tent ceremony"
described by George Nelson. The instrument was seen to obey the demands
of the spirit world rather than its corporeal player: "'Give me my rattler' (said
one of the older) 'that I sing &C; it may happen that we find grace.' He
sang and shook his rattler, but it would not sound. After frequent repeated
trials to no effect he became vexed and threw it out of doors to the Dogs"
(Nelson 1988, 77–78). In 1743, James Isham also described the use of a
rattle: "where was abou't 30 Indians very merry Dispos'd with two old
men, one Drumming on a piece of parchment tied on an o'n Kettle,—the

other with a st'k like a Ratle, with parchmt. On both sides, and shott or stones on the inside to make itt Ratle, asking the Reason of all this seeming mirth,—one made answer itt was a goose feas't as they styl' itt."

In 1930, John M. Cooper described two other instruments among the northern Algonquians that produced powerful sounds and were used in conjunction with song. Both assisted in bringing the cold north wind to form a crust on the ice that made travel by snowshoe and toboggan easier. The first was the buzzer, made of a bark, wooden, or bone disc to which two parallel strings were attached. The disc was revolved with a twirling motion and the strings were alternately loosened and held taut, causing the disc to rotate with a loud buzzing noise. The second instrument, found throughout the world, was the bullroarer. The Algonquians made this from a flat almond-shaped piece of wood with a string attached. Holding the string, they twirled the bullroarer around their head making a whirring sound. These two sound-makers were also noted by Flannery (1936).

The Cree hunters did not think of their drums and rattles as musical instruments but as integral parts of their hunting life. These were tools that facilitated communication with the world of unseen living beings. When he wished the drum to talk to him, the Cree hunter sang into it, merging his voice with the drum vibrations. Edward Ottereyes, a Cree man from Nemiscau, southeast of Chisasibi, said (1983): "The drum could give them the spirit while they held it in their hand. The drum could hear the singer while he's singing." Mr. Ottereyes then related a story about two elders who sang and drummed all night during a very bad storm. The following day the hunter with the drum went out and came back with a lot of caribou meat. He concluded, "When the elders gather together, by using the drum, sometimes they can see what they're going to kill when they hunt. They can see ahead of them." Certainly the Christian missionaries knew the role of the drum in Cree mental life, for in the past it was a major target of their proselytizing.

Nowadays, the Cree of Chisasibi use none of these instruments in their original magical context. Joseph Rupert, a man in his seventies in 1984, told me that the drum was already gone when his grandfather died, but they continued to sing. Even though the tangible objects are rarely seen, the stories and beliefs about the drum remain firmly in the minds of the old people. William Jack (1982) said, "They had great powers years ago—the drumming helped them a lot." Abraham Martinhunter (1984) stated, "The drums are extinct now. They used to use drums with the song." Samson Lameboy told how an old man had fallen ill because of the sorcery of an *Inuk*, and "started banging the drum and recovered from the illness caused by the Inuk" (1982). In fact, the old man was able to transfer the spell back to the Inuk, who then fell ill and died. The drumming was attendant to the occasion and essential to the recovery. Samson Lameboy concluded his story by saying: "The drums were very powerful at that time."

The Goose Dance

In the early 1980s, a few Manitoba elders could remember the settings for the songs and drums and give detailed accounts of the once-important ceremony known as the goose dance. This Cree ceremony showed respect and love for the spirit being of the geese. The geese were commemorated by the smoking of the pipe, by prayers, and by proper handling and eating of ducks and geese. In 1981, elder Roddy Garrick described his memories of going to a goose dance as a child. He said the dances were held in fall and spring, when the geese were overhead. Adults and children danced, and infants were cared for by old people. He recalled a large, circular, unroofed palisade constructed from thick poles about seven feet long that were stuck into the ground. A big fire was built in the centre for cooking the geese and ducks. For special ceremonies, the food was spread out on white sheets, and at all times it was important that no food be dropped on the ground. Tobacco was placed around the fire, and there was a tub of pipes of different shapes and sizes from which to choose. Mr. Garrick believed that the smoking had a religious element to it, although he heard no prayers. He said that the men loved to smoke and the dancing place was like a smokestack!

He described how they danced around the circle of the palisade. The lead dancer looked at his lady and imitated the honk of a goose; she would then jump up and join him in the dance. Then another man would get up and call to his lady.[3] When all were up and the dance was complete, they would leave the circle as they entered it. The leader was the last to sit.

During the dance, a drum was played continuously by the same two men, who took turns beating. Often the drums were suspended by a long cord from the ceiling for playing. The drummers smoked and ate, but didn't dance. Only the men sang, and although Mr. Garrick thought the singers were telling a story, he couldn't tell what they were saying.

Roddy Garrick's reminiscence of the northern Manitoba goose dance conforms well to accounts such as those by anthropologist David Meyer. Unfortunately, there are few details about the songs of this vanished ceremony: their sound, their words, or their form. We do have an Ojibwe song included in a myth, "Wisahkecahk and the Shut-Eye Dancers," which is also a favourite of the Cree. I include it below (fig. 1.2) as a possible example of the sort of song one might have heard from the Manitoba Cree. In 1910, musicologist Frances Densmore recorded it under the title "Song of Wenabojo," sung by an Ojibwe named Gatcitcigicig who lived on the shore of Lake Superior.[4]

David Meyer (1990, 11) believes the prevalence of the trickster story of "Wisahkecahk and the Shut-Eye Dancers" is confirmation of the centrality of the goose dance in Cree culture. The story, told by both the Cree and Ojibwe, is as follows: Wisahkecahk the trickster (Wenabojo, in Ojibwe) invited various kinds of waterfowl, geese, ducks, and loons to a feast. In some variants, he attracted these curious animals by putting his songs in a bag on his back. Then Wisahkecahk invited them to close their eyes and dance. While he sang and the geese danced, he wrung their necks one by one, saying, "There is going to be a feast, all right!" Unfortunately for the trickster, one duck happened to open his eyes, and then many of the survivors fled. Frances Densmore wrote:

> Before beginning the song, the singer said, "I am arranging to have a dance, my little brothers and sisters." After the first rendition he said, "Dance, dance, dance faster, my little brothers and sisters." This is mentioned to show the custom of interspersing the renditions of the song with short speeches. (Densmore 1910, 206)

The original dialect as recorded by Densmore appears in figure 1.2.

Densmore noted that Anishnabe singers tried to achieve a vibrato or wavering tone while they sang and that most of these songs would be accompanied by either the drum or the rattle. As we shall see, these are general characteristics of Cree song. In 1994, I recorded a Manitoba teacher of Ojibwe, Charles Beauchamp, singing this song while playing his hand drum, and for fun he changed the syllables *yu we he he* to *quack-quack quack quack*!

We know also that the roles of men and women in the music of the ceremony varied according to circumstances, such as the age of the woman. In describing one ceremony that took place in a tent, Meyer remarks that women were not allowed inside (1990, 4); in another ceremony, however, women both drummed and sang (14), roles usually reserved for respected men. Women typically participated in the music only as dancers, as in the following account:

> As soon as the guests have eaten their fill, they cover the remaining food, and dancing commences around the fire. While men and women join the circling dancers to imitate the wildfowl in actions and calls, a conjuror who sits near the wall sings and beats a primitive rhythm on his drum. (Mason 1967, 60)

	Translation
Onakaowin Nenapos	**Song of Wenabojo**
Keko win inapikekwan	**Don't look**
Kekamameskwac	**Or you will all take**
Ki ka cikwenikom	**Your turns at getting your necks wrung.**

Figure 1.2: "Song of Wenabojo" (Onakaowin Nenapos), sung by Gatcitcigicig. Also sung by Charles Beauchamp, Peguis, Manitoba

The singing and drumming was an important guide for the participants in the goose dance ceremony, as noted in the 1850s by the Reverend Henry Budd, who established Neepoweewin Mission across the Saskatchewan River from the Hudson's Bay Company Fort à la Corne post. He noted that after the ceremonial lodge was completed on the first of April, the drum was heard throughout the night. The next day the Cree arrived for ten intensive days of feasting and dancing. The ceremony not only began but ended with the drumming and singing (Meyer 1990, 4). Moreover, the drums controlled the progress of the ceremony. For example, when the drumming began, the dancers were expected to dance, and when the drumming stopped, they quit the dance:

> The last dance of the ceremony was preceded by a speech in which the ceremonial leader invited the wolf to visit the lodge after the people had left and to take any morsels of food which had been left behind. The leader then sang a wolf song and as the dancers performed they all, men, women, and children lifted their heads and howled from time to time. When this song ended, so did the ceremony. (Meyer 1990, 14)

Healing Songs

I heard few memories of old songs used specifically for healing, although they certainly did form an integral part of healing in the past. In his 1823 journal, George Nelson made specific reference to the use of songs and a rattler to aid a dying woman at a feast:

Every thing being prepared, the guests were just going to eat when the feast-man's mother dropped suddenly as if dead: everyone was struck with consternation. They had recourse to their medicines, songs, rattlers, &c, as usual; at last he fell to sucking his mother in one of her temples: suddenly they heard something "crack": the Indian drew back, his mother arose perfectly recovered and all became well. (Nelson 1988, 64)

Healing songs were also sung in the sweat lodge, although many believe the sweat lodge to be a more recent introduction in the subarctic. In northern Quebec, elders recall heating up rocks to warm the body of a sick person (Sam Visitor, 1984). Similarly in a sweat lodge ceremony, water is poured on hot rocks to produce steam and make people sweat. An elder usually guides the event, which may include prayers, songs, and a prescribed entry and exit. Several years ago, when I attended a "sweat" in northern Manitoba, I heard songs, all by men, with the intense vocal quality and distinctive descending phrases of Plains music. Yet the songs were sung strongly and with conviction by these northern Cree. (In a later chapter, we shall read about the northerners' interest in southern culture, particularly Ojibwe song. The Ojibwe, in turn, acquired many of their songs from peoples farther south, such as the Dakota.)

Although most of the old songs are gone, the belief in Indian medicine lives on. Roddy Garrick said that healers were never formally trained in healing, but gained knowledge by dreaming; the trees and plants talked to the healer in his dreams. Tobacco was left at the tree where one got the medicine (Betsy Wolanski 1981). George Nelson said that each root and herb had an appropriate song.

Roots and herbs also, i.e., such as are medicinal, appear, and teach their votaries their respective Songs—how they must do, what ceremonies they must perform in taking them out of the Ground, their different applications, &c, &c. But these roots, herbs &c (medecins), tho' they appear in their Dreams, they do not shew themselves in the Conjuring Hut, box or frame, that I learn. (Nelson 1988, 38)

The people I met believed that all plants have some kind of medicine, but not all people could use the same kind. Native doctors will teach a patient how to make the medicine they are given, but will not give the information to just anyone who asks, particularly white people. In the past, the white authorities have threatened healers with jail and confiscated their medicine bags. In response, healers either hid their medicines or ceased to make them; as a consequence of the latter response, many healing songs and their words were forgotten.

Song in Hunting Ceremonies

In a Cree hunter's life, the songs and rituals are limited largely to the hunt and the animals, athough the hunters recalled young girls singing about their boyfriends and young men singing about their girls. William Jack (1982) said jokingly, "Now I don't hear the young ladies sing about their boyfriends. Maybe they do it in English, so I don't understand."

Flannery observed, "Even the crises of life—birth, adolescence, marriage, and death—are entirely or almost entirely unmarked by religious or magical observances" (1936, 54). Instead, Cree ceremony marked hunting events. In June 1984 I observed a walking-out ceremony, held to celebrate the first independent steps of a child on the ground outside. A special tent was erected for the ceremony, which was held for three children. Each carried a miniature tool carved from wood, the boys a bow and arrow or gun, and the girl an axe, needed for the hunting life. The children were guided by a parent clockwise around an oval-shaped path that led from the tent to the outdoors and back to the interior of the tent, where each child was greeted affectionately by the parents. Afterwards a large feast was attended by all the members of the children's family.

The elders did not recall the singing of any songs at this ceremony, but one elder played a cassette recording of a local hunter's traditional hunting song. They did recall songs to celebrate a youth's first catch (*aschchig-othwa gomit nikamon*), but these were never recorded.

Other special-occasion songs were sung during the game feasts, celebrations held in the spring by the Mistassini Cree, which anthropologist Frank Speck described as "somewhat formal." These game feasts are reminiscent of the Manitoba Goose Dance. A special tent facing the southeast was constructed. Inside, an old man drummed and sang while the guests ate pemmican (dry reindeer meat mixed with fat and marrow). The women were invited to eat the remains after the men had eaten. After two days, the feast ended and a dance began. No food was allowed out of the tent for fear that the deer would all desert the area, causing starvation among the people. For the same reason, dogs were not allowed near the food, and all the bones were pounded and burned (Speck 1935, 200). Adrian Tanner interpreted the drumming and singing at Mistassini feasts as forms of offerings, "intended specifically to ensure successful future hunting ... most often performed at feasts early in the season" (1979, 165).

Many of the Cree in Chisasibi have little recollection of these traditional feasts, the feast song *migoshaw nikamon*, or the significance of the feast for the hunt. The feast that followed the walking-out ceremony in Chisasibi, to which I was invited, was a hasty event, with no narrative. After consuming huge quantities of wild meats, bannock, cake, and tea, the guests quickly left, but not before filling plastic bags with the remaining food, so that none was left. In 1984, Edward Ottereyes recalled the old feasts as follows:

The feast, they all gather in a circle
They put the beaver head in the middle
And cover it with a cloth
They don't touch it until the drum is used
All the elders gather around the drum and sing
They would take turns playing the drum made of caribou hide
They hung the drum from the tipi, then began to sing
After they drum and sing, then they have the feast

Robert Brightman describes an "Eat-All Feast" in 1977 at Watt Lake in northern Manitoba. He was invited to *wihkohtowin*, a "feast of game at which a large surplus is prepared and entirely consumed" (2002, 214). The cabin was cleaned, the participants dressed up, and, in a separate cooking tent, two large kettles were filled with four beavers, and another with macaroni and cheese. After the cooked meat was brought in, and the tipi door shut, the hunter thanked his father, his wife, the beavers, and other animals he had trapped. He asked that the guests try to eat all the food that had been prepared.

After the cleanup, Marcel extracted a suitcase from under the bed and removed a single-headed drum perhaps two inches in depth and two feet in diameter. The drum was given to Antoine who held it vertically in front of him, drumming with a carved stick, and singing so softly that I could not have understood him even if the words had been English. The drum passed successively to Marcel and to Edouard, each of whom sang softly while the others smoked and talked. (Brightman 2002, 217)

The Shaking Tent: A Sound Event

Much of Cree spiritual power is shown in the shaking tent ceremony, called *goshabichikan nohhekan* in East Cree. (In western Cree dialects it is called *kosapahcikan*, which now means "television," an appropriate shift of meaning, for in both instances you would be seeing things.) This event is no longer regularly practised in Quebec or Manitoba, but the deeds performed by the shamans in the tent are a favourite subject for those older persons who remember and respect the powers the Cree had in past times. The shaking tent ceremony is enacted by a shaman with magical powers seeking knowledge, usually about the future. For example, if the shaman was old, he might wish to know how much longer he would live. "The man would question the voice and would ask for whatever he came for, such as better weather, health, hunting," explained Sam Visitor (1982). "It seemed like the person was just going to the government for this and that."

Abraham Martinhunter (1984) said: "The songs gave them power when they used the little hut," a point also made by Samson Lameboy (1982): "When they had their tents, when they were using their powers, they could see where they could kill the game." In her 1995 study, Ellen Smallboy added another interpretation, describing the shaking tent as an "indirect forum for group expression of group disapproval since Cree tended to avoid direct criticism of others not in family group" (19).

A dome-shaped tent was erected specially for the event. It held only one person, and my translator referred to it as "the little hut," perhaps referring to its dome shape. In the tent, the shaman communicated through prayer and song (*goshabichikan nohhekan*) with his *mistapeo* (the spirit person within each human), and with other spirit beings who would give him information. There was usually an audience for this ceremony, and the events usually began at twilight. The shaman would drum and sing, asking multiple *ahcak* (spirits) to join him. The invisible spirits entered through the opening in the top of the tent, which would shake visibly and audibly as they entered and exited. Community members witnessed the shaking of the tent and heard the conversation within the tent between the shaman and his *mistapeo*, who talked and sang in different voices.

Because the shaman performed inside the little hut and was not seen, his communication with the audience was mainly through sound. The spirits, including those of animals, existed vocally for the audience, through their spoken languages. Brightman says the characters are identified by their "songs, choice of linguistic code, paralinguistic effects, and typified genres, taking the latter to refer to particular topics and styles of discourse" (2002, 172).

The sound of the shaking-tent songs differs considerably from that of the hunting songs, yet in common with the hunting songs they show great individual differences in performance. The shaking tent songs resemble the hypnotic, chant-like sounds of much religious music. In Harvey Feit's recording of Andrew Ottereyes of Waswanipi, Quebec, only one durational value is used, in contrast to the rhythmic variety in the hunting songs. The pitch is a repetitive monotone; the hunting songs are melodic. Yet the Cree sound ideal holds firm: the shaking of the tent sounds much like the shaking of the rattle, and both are used when communicating with the spirits and in times of transition or uncertainty.

The shaking tent songs were sung using syllables and contained words, but these words were obscured by the singer. In Feit's 1969 transcript of the shaking-tent ceremony, the spoken words are written out, but the translators, Joseph and Eve Ottereyes, state that they cannot understand them. Indeed, the transcript shows the singer carefully explaining what he is singing (in this specific case, it was a song about someone called Johnny Grant, and another song about the bear). Feit recorded that "Mr. Ottereyes repeated one song in ordinary speech in case we did not understand him" (Feit 1983, 4).

In another shaking-tent ceremony recorded in 1965 by Richard Preston, in the same decade as the one described above, I hear a different melodic contour.[5] The singer, Joseph Cheezo, slides down an interval of a fifth upon each repetition of the song's pattern. The last note repeated many times becomes a lengthy tail. Occasionally, several different pitches are inserted into the tail, so that it becomes tunelike. The syllables are clear, and change upon repetition of phrases, but again the words are apparently untranslatable. Like Mr. Ottereyes' shaking-tent song, Mr. Cheezo's has a regular percussive background for the sung pitches. Both have a similar vocal timbre.

Manitoba elders shared with me their vivid memories of the shaking tent itself. Roddy Garrick described how he saw the tipi constructed and tied so as to be entirely solid, but then saw the structure move when the old shaman inside was singing. He described another elder who went to another shaking-tent ceremony at Cross Lake, Manitoba, to which two white men were invited from the local Hudson's Bay Company post. The white men had not believed in the shaking tent, but when they saw it with their own eyes, they decided to fetch their preacher. When the preacher arrived, however, the tent stopped shaking (Wolanski 1981).

SONGS ABOUT THE SHAKING TENT

The shaking tent is remembered in song as well as story. Below are two songs about the shaking tent that are musically similar to his other hunting songs.

The first East Cree song below describes a young man's ability to kill deer through his knowledge of the shaking tent; the second is about a young man and his father communicating through the powers of the shaking tent.

> The song is about a young hunter and his knowledge of the shaking
> tent
> How he can kill the deer, through using the shaking tent. (George
> Pepabano)

This is a song about a young man singing about his father
Who had supernatural powers through the shaking tent
The young man had the same thing too so he's singing about it
They both had powers
That is how they communicate with each other. (George Pepabano)

Songs, Sounds, and Silence

The context for Cree song is the people's life in the bush, where every sound is significant. Their traditional mode of subsistence is bound up with the natural sounds around them. Successful hunting depends upon effective use of sounds, and equally on the use of silence. Robert Potts (1982) stressed the fact that he would never sing when he was busy doing work in the bush for fear of forewarning the animals. Samson Lameboy (1984) made the following point:

The fox is very, very smart.
You have to be very, very silent.
The fox can hear you and then you lose him
even when he is far, far away
some make mouse sounds, or muskrat sounds,
if you make these sounds, they'll come running to you.

Many of the sounds of nature were attributed with special meaning and with specific usages related to the hunt. Adrian Tanner (1979, 109 and 146) noted that, to the Mistassini hunter, the song of the Canada Jay meant hunting success; the crackling of a fire was a predictor of a future kill; and whistling (*kwisgoshiw*, in East Cree) was disapproved of because it could cause strong winds.

George Nelson observed that children also learned how sounds could harm as well as heal: "Their horror of the Devil is so great, that no one ever utters it but when unavoidable; and if thro' inadvertency or ignorance one of their children should mention it, he is severely reprimanded by all who hear" (1988, 37).

The James Bay stories (*tipaachimoon*) abound with references to song, sound, and silence or absence of human-made sound. Many of them emphasize the importance of silence as a protection against bad spirits: for example, whenever an *atosh* (giant) was thought to be in the vicinity, people would stay inside the tipi and not make a sound, even though they were very scared. The approach of the evil being was signalled by the sound of footsteps close to the tipi. Children were told to keep quiet, not to move around, and women were instructed just to gather wood, not to chop it. These stories, excerpted below, show us the immense power of sounds:

That night they heard a sound coming from far away—like someone screaming—a sound they had never heard before; a scream they could not describe. (Martinhunter 1982)

As the story continues, the encounter with the *atosh* is full of references to frightening sounds:

Then they heard something going by the tipi
there was a lot of commotion—seagulls, scraping, different sounds
they heard something in the sky, so went out again
after they came in, they heard a thump outside the door.

Abraham Martinhunter's wife, Daisy, told a story in which evil was known through sound:

The two young girls were gathering twigs for the fire
All the time he kept telling them not to say a word
Just to keep quiet if they hear anything or a noise.
They used to say, whenever a giant used to meet people inland
In the olden days he used to go toward a tipi from the west side.
That's what the legend told.
The old man told them, "Pretty soon now you will hear something."
It was dark now
They could hear a sound coming toward the tipi
A sound of footsteps like something very heavy
Breaking the bush and trees along the way.
They didn't make a sound even though they were very afraid
Then the sound of footsteps was so close to the tipi
The canoes were on each side of the tipi
They could hear
That someone was touching the side of one of the canoes
As if the hand was very coarse
Someone was touching the canoe from the other end
Going toward the door of the tipi.
They could tell by the sound of the coarse hand
That he was getting very close to the door touching the canoe
Then the old man, he had a gun
In the past, whenever the giant used to destroy people
The gun never used to go off
He put the gun on one of the poles of the tipi
The old woman whispered "ka" in a frightened tone
Because the sound coming from outside on the canoe
Was going toward the doorway of the tipi now.
The old man pulled the trigger of the gun, the shot went off
After the shot they heard nothing
Not even the sound of the rapids of the waterfall

It was very quiet, slowly the sound of the water came back
Before the sound of the rapids
Then shortly after they hear the sound up in the skies
Of all kinds of birds and fowl making sounds.
That was after the shot
Then after, the old man told them, light the fire of the tipi
And we'll drink some tea, then we will go to bed. (Daisy Martinhunter
1982)

The *atosh* is better known as a *witiko*. *Witikos* are people who become crazed from famine, losing all control over their behaviour, and who sometimes request their own execution. These naked, dirty creatures become cannibalistic, and it's believed they gain the power of the victims they eat. Because they pose real danger, the community must be rid of them, as in the following story told by William Jack:

> To rid the camp of the fearful *atosh*, the old man asked for a bowl of water and white cloth. He put the cloth over his head and looked into the water to find out what was frightening them. Then he started singing into the water. He got up and went out of the tipi, singing louder and louder—as if the singing was way up in the air. Finally the old man was able to have the monster bound up in a heavy chain and dropped into the middle of a lake. (Jack 1982)

Thus, song was essential for spiritual as well as physical protection. Nelson wrote that nearly all Saulteaux or Cree youths were initiated by seeking a dream in which a "man," who later assumed his proper form as any living thing (for example, a fish or a plant such as a tree) would address the youth: "Now don't you remember my song? Whenever you will wish to call upon me, sing this song, and I shall not be far—I will come and do for you what you require" (1988, 35). Hence, by singing a song, the youth acquired a spirit protector.

These, then, are the settings for the old songs. They were essential to daily hunting life and to ceremonies in which people sought to know the future, to be healed, and to be assured of hunting success.

2

Song and History

This chapter focuses on the music relationship between the Cree and Europeans through four centuries and shows the challenges to the survival of old Cree song. Before beginning, it should be noted that other Native groups, particularly the Ojibwe, also influenced Cree song, and in the final chapter you shall see how Plains powwow has become a subarctic Cree music. Native music exchanges were accelerated by the displacement of many peoples brought about by European pressures for furs and land. Doubtless there had always been song exchanges between groups, but Native musics were brought together, and songs carried across the continent, at a rate hitherto unexperienced. Those individuals with facility in speaking both the Algonquian and English languages were of crucial importance to trade, both of objects and ideas. That is a subject worthy of independent investigation. The question for this study, however, is how Native music has changed as a result of contact with non-Natives. What European music did the Cree hear? How were the new sounds brought to them? How did all this affect their music practices?

Europeans moved people and goods efficiently with their large ships and they organized fur convoys, but, until the missionaries, they were less concerned about transmitting information to the indigenous peoples. The Cree were immediately attracted to essential material items such as European pots and knives, but for nearly two hundred years they exhibited little interest in European ways. Indeed, the European newcomers had more need of Cree knowledge than the Cree had of European. But the Cree did willingly embrace European fiddle music, and they made it their own.

European music arrived in the New World at first contact. Song, story, and dance were vital to the well-being of sailors on-board ship, and many of the shanties (the word comes from the French *chanter*) have become North American standards.[1] Whalers, too, sang shanties to help them endure years at a time of rough life on awkward tub-boats that stank of whale oil. The Inuit, northern neighbours of the Cree, acquired from these whalers the button accordion and square dance. The eastern Cree also have knowledge of the accordion, and have developed their own word for a "pushing and pulling instrument": *kashehischbitaakanowiich*. Perhaps they learned this instrument from the Inuit as well as from the whalers, because after 1840 the Inuit came regularly to Chisasibi to trade fox furs, seal blubber, and caribou skins. On the west side of Hudson Bay, the Cree may have had less exposure to shipboard music, because the ships were anchored several miles offshore at bay ports such as York Factory. This was necessitated by the dangers of going aground on the silt deposits at the mouths of the rivers flowing into James Bay. Furthermore, the west coast of the bay offered no "grog" shops to attract sailors to land.

Ships frequently carried a small assortment of percussion and brass instruments. Chappell, in 1817, described the reaction of a Cree chief taken on board the HMS Rosamond in the following way: "He appeared a very intelligent man, and was highly delighted with everything he saw on board the ship. He was not particularly pleased with any of our musical instruments, except the drum" (Chappell 1817, 201). It is likely that his reaction was typical; historians such as Daniel Francis and Toby Morantz (1983) have noted that the Cree did not indiscriminately embrace everything European. As long as they were materially independent, they sought items that had direct utility for their subsistence lifestyle. In similar fashion, they adopted only the European music and instruments that sustained their culture.

This history of Cree song focuses on British music, because exposure in the north to French music, such as the voyageur songs, was sporadic. With the exception of exploratory trips into the north, the French were generally confined to fur-trading routes that crossed southern Canada. The first recorded meeting of the James Bay Cree with the British occurred in 1611, with the ill-fated Henry Hudson, who was seeking a northwest passage to the Orient.[2] We know that one Cree man boarded Hudson's ship and conducted trade: two deer and two beaver skins in return for a knife, a looking glass, and buttons. Then, in the summer of 1668, English sponsors, advised by Radisson and Groseilliers, sent a ship, the *Nonsuch*, to collect furs from the area around Charles Fort. It is known that the *Nonsuch* had a trumpet aboard, perhaps for signalling. The *Nonsuch* crew, captained by Zachariah Gillam and Groseilliers, remained in the area and established trading posts for regular bartering of furs. Their efforts were rewarded when, in the spring of 1669, three hundred families arrived with furs, which were sent back to England that very summer. So impressed were the Cree that they told stories about the *Nonsuch* for the next hundred years. That

October, a second ship, the *Wivenhoe*, arrived at James Bay after visiting the mouth of the Nelson River. The ship's crew wintered over, using old sails to cover their wigwam. They were absolutely dependent upon the local population for food, mostly deer, fowl, and rabbits; hence, the Cree were frequent visitors among the white men.

From 1672 on, Charles Fort, later named Rupert House, was occupied year round by Hudson's Bay Company men. By 1679, the Hudson's Bay Company had three more fur-trading posts on the major rivers at the south end of James Bay. By this time, the Indians were enthusiastic visitors because they wanted and needed guns, ammunition, and metal implements, such as cooking pots. Only after these were obtained would they trade for luxuries such as brandy, tobacco, beads, combs, and mirrors. Relations between the two groups were cordial, as dictated by their mutual dependency. In fact, two Cree men agreed to travel to London. One died during the sea voyage; the other, named Attash, returned home the next spring. In contrast, the French–English rivalry for the Native supply of furs was far from cordial. For the most part, the French confined their trade to inland areas and were more active in going out to meet the Indians, while the English waited to receive furs at their posts on James Bay. Trade continued in this fashion until the eighteenth century; the only major development in the meantime was the escalating rivalry between the French and English, and the increased bartering of brandy to ensure Indian trade.

The frequent exchanges in the seventeenth century were generally brief and businesslike. The inland trading groups stayed at the post for only a few days, just enough time to trade and rest between journeys. If a large group arrived, a ceremony might be held in which the postmaster and leading Indians would give speeches, smoke a pipe, and exchange gifts. The furs would be presented, then the Cree hunters would depart, for they did not bring their families. Nor were they encouraged to linger by company employees, who feared that the hunters would become dependent upon the company food stores. Moreover, company employees were forbidden to fraternize with the Cree, to discourage private trading.

We have little record of northern Cree reaction to British song, but a Récollet priest, Gabriel Sagard, writing about the Natives he encountered in New France, noted that they enjoyed the ritual music of the church. On the other hand, these Natives "expressed repugnance at the profane and dissolute songs of the French" (Amtmann 1975, 63). Sagard explains the affinity of Natives for church music as the result of the similarity between traditional Native and religious music, believing that "the sensuous melodic, harmonic, and rhythmic structure of the French chanson was too different from traditional Native song" (63). Alfred G. Bailey describes seventeenth-century Native music in the south as follows:

> It is probable, however, that the drum remained the chief musical instrument of the Indians, although the French had violins, flutes and organs, at Quebec in the seventeenth century. These were in use in the dramatic rituals of the church to which the Indians were often willing accessories. (Bailey 1969, 156)

The unilingual Cree elders in the 1980s generally confirm this penchant for Christian hymns and lack of interest in other Euro-American music, with the exception of fiddle music, largely because they couldn't understand the words to secular Euro-American song.

During the first decades of the eighteenth century, visits by inland Cree to the posts became more regular; in fact, the Company authorities assigned families to particular trading posts, which restricted their traditional freedom of movement. Moreover, some remained for the summer months and came to be called "homeguard Indians." They supplied the post with food, especially geese and fish, and in return received luxury items such as brandy and tobacco. To ensure supply, staples were traded only for fur. By the 1760s, a few families remained longer to knit snowshoes and nets. They became the first hunters to be employees of the Company.

The posts were manned by the British working classes: sailors who doubled as general labourers, as well as tradesmen such as tailors, gunsmiths, bricklayers, and carpenters. Music instruments such as the fiddle, zither, harmonica, and fife were part of the daily life of the posts as early as the seventeenth century, as were folk songs sung by company labourers. As stated earlier, these men were forbidden to socialize with the Indian population, particularly the women, but this policy was often ignored, especially by the postmasters, a number of whom had Cree wives and families. By the last half of the eighteenth century, many company servants were of mixed blood. Given this level of interaction, the Cree must have heard the white people's music, even though the companies discouraged participation by Native people, for the fear that any change in Cree society might disrupt the flow of furs to the posts. In the eighteenth century, the Cree may have experienced a different kind of music with the arrival of more literate tradesmen. Still, there is no indication that secular song held any interest for the independent Cree. We hear only about their learning sacred music, as in the following account written by Henry Ellis in 1748: "They acknowledge a Being of infinite Goodness ... They likewise sing a kind of Hymn in his Praise, and this in a grave solemn Tone, not altogether disagreeable" (Ellis 1748, 193).

By the late eighteenth century, the postmasters relied more and more upon the Indians as guides and voyageurs, as the British tried to extend their trade inland to counteract French and other independent competitors. The other European peoples sometimes cut off the flow of furs to the coastal trading posts. Another contribution from the Indians was the canoe, used for the transportation of furs.[3] This, of course, meant that work for the company was replacing subsistence activities among the Indians, causing their families to spend more time closer to the posts, especially during the summer, when the men were away with the canoe brigades. Even the lives of the Cree remote from the post were regularized by the exact accounting system adopted by the Hudson's Bay Company, which ensured that they always traded at the same post.

By the nineteenth century, the Cree had become an essential part of trading-post operation, and some Cree even supervised posts. Increasingly, men were hired for non-traditional work, such as transporting and cutting hay. Women, too, were employed to trap game, fish, and gather berries. Homeguard Indians, those who lived permanently at the posts, often made up more than one half of the full-time post employees, and a large proportion were of mixed blood. Indeed, the Company hoped that these Natives and mixed-bloods would eventually replace the European recruits, who were often ill suited to the rigours of northern life. Yet despite the changes described above, subsistence activities remained essentially unaltered for most Cree, even for those who were hired at the post for the summer months. In September, they hunted goose, and after that, fishing resumed. At snowfall, the families went to their own hunting grounds, and in spring, the goose hunt began again.

By 1867, Fort George (Chisasibi) was a thriving trading post, and relied so much upon Cree workers that the Hudson Bay employees began to take an interest in educating the Native children, teaching them religion, reading, and writing. This was a reversal of earlier policy designed to keep the Cree as trappers. These coastal Cree of the late nineteenth century developed familiarity with the sound of European music. And the introduction of print to communicate information was a significant change to a group who used exclusively oral transmission of knowledge.

Missionary Influence

In the nineteenth century, Christian missionaries began work in a sustained way, in both northern Quebec and Manitoba. Their intent was to convert all Cree to Christianity, and song was an important means to this end. They did not want Cree furs; they wanted Cree souls.

Missionaries received a mixed reception from both Native and non-Native people in the North. They were employed by the Hudson's Bay Company, but company employees disliked the priests' interference in Native life. For example, the missionaries proscribed the use of drums by Cree people, which irritated the white traders because it interfered with the established pattern of fur production and trading. An example of the friction between church and company is evident in the following statement by a Cree who worked as a guide: "We used to bring the ministers along the coast. The minister wouldn't go on the boat, [so] we would bring them by canoe. [The Company] wouldn't let the minister go on the boat. I took them to Great Whale to get people married and baptized" (Martinhunter 1982).

Missionaries taught the Cree to read, and they provided a writing system so that the Cree could read their own Algonquian language. To this end, they used the system of writing with syllabics developed by James Evans in 1840, in Norway House, Manitoba. Of course, this was a powerful tool for teaching and spreading Christianity, but it was also the introduction of a new way to communicate, and, as we shall see, the Cree took to it readily.

The Cree music practices in Manitoba's north were among the first to change, due to the easy access provided to outside influences by the waterways, such as the Hayes River flowing into Hudson Bay, and especially Lake Winnipeg, an enormous inland lake. In comparing land to water travel, Reverend Egerton R. Young, who began his work in northern Manitoba in 1868, wrote: "The travelling on [Lake] Winnipeg was mere child's play to what followed after we had plunged into the forest country" (1893, 111). By the early nineteenth century, the Red River settlement near the southern tip of Lake Winnipeg was a stopping-off point for travellers proceeding in all directions. Because of the lake, trappers and missionaries had access to the north. Travel by water facilitated the exchange of ideas and goods between Red River and York Factory. From here, goods, mostly from London, England, were taken "up south" (a term still used in isolated communities along the river) by heavy boats to Norway House, through a system of lakes and rivers known as the "Hayes River route." Norway House, established in 1814 by the Hudson's Bay Company at the northern edge of Lake Winnipeg, was the great distribution centre for posts such as Cross Lake, Cross Portage, Nelson House, Poplar River, and Berens River. In spring, boat brigades came with their furs from the inland posts down the river to Norway House. The furs were packed and inventoried to be sent by boat to York Factory in the late summer, then shipped to London for auction. Local tripmen were employed to carry freight to these places and also to Red

River. By the 1830s, a number of Cree had regular employment fishing, haying, and cutting wood for Norway House, and they began to settle their families in a Cree village near the post.

Because of its accessibility by water from both the south and the north, Norway House prospered as a fur-trade centre and, afterwards, as the site of the first Methodist mission in Western Canada. When rail transportation farther south improved, the fur trade business in Norway House declined, but the mission continued to grow. By 1875, Reverend George Young, D. D., visiting Norway House from the Red River settlement, was able to report the following:

> The Rossville Mission is very pleasantly situated on the shore of a beautiful little lake, within two miles of Norway House Post, and is the oldest and by far the strongest of our Indian missions in the North-west. It was established in 1840 by the Rev. Mr. Rundle, Wesleyan missionary from London. In looking over the register of baptisms and marriages, which has been carefully kept from the first, I found the first baptism recorded on the 28th day of May, 1840, by Mr. Rundle, and the last on the 3d of January, 1875, by myself. Between these Dates one thousand five hundred and sixty baptisms were registered. Mr. Rundle was succeeded by the late Rev. James Evans, who, in labours and travels and successes, was 'more abundant' and whose name is ever mentioned by these Christian Indians with profoundest respect and gratitude. Probably one thousand Indians or more consider this place, and neighbourhoods adjacent, their home. The mission itself embraces a large number of families who live in very comfortable and clean-looking little houses, not far from the church and school and mission house. The church, which has been enlarged once, was built by Mr. Evans, and is at present about sixty feet by forty feet, and, as it is closely seated, I suppose contains occasionally some four hundred, little and big, of a congregation. (Young 1897, 293)

Among the dedicated immigrants was the brilliant linguist James Evans (1801–46), the son of a sea captain whose family emigrated to Canada. He married Mary Blithe Smith and began his work as a teacher. After he was ordained, he wrote that his motivation was to "save souls by preaching and travelling and visiting the poor heathen in their wretched wigwams, and teaching young and old the way of life" (Fast 1983, 77–78). He served at Norway House, Manitoba, where he established missions, preached, and taught school. More so than many of his colleagues, Evans adapted to the Cree lifestyle and tried to bridge the gap between Indian belief and Christianity.

Literacy, to enable the reading of the Bible, was basic to Protestant Christianity. To this end, James Evans provided the Cree in 1840 with syllabics, a practical writing system which represented the sounds of Cree, and then translated and printed portions of hymns and scripture into the syllabic system (see fig. 4.1). Other missionaries took up this system. In 1858, William Mason, with his Cree-speaking wife, went to England, where the couple worked on translations of the Bible into syllabics. By 1861, the entire Scriptures were available in Cree syllabics (Fast 1983, 187). The syllabics were carried from Manitoba to the Quebec Cree, and eventually used by the Inuit, who translated the texts into a similar syllabic system that represented their language.[4]

The missionary intent was to preach the Christian religion, but missionaries were also, perhaps even more so, revolutionizing communication. Of course, syllabics were a powerful tool for teaching and spreading Christianity, but they also provided a new way to communicate, and the Cree took to it readily. When asked if he took his prayer book to the bush, an elder replied, "I take it with me wherever I go" (Martinhunter 1984). A powerful new way to transmit knowledge had been introduced to the northern peoples: the Cree could now read and write their own Algonquian language.

Even before the arrival of syllabics in Quebec, many Cree were well acquainted with Christianity and prepared to be baptized and married. From the time the first resident Anglican missionary arrived in Fort George in 1852, until the 1970s, the Christian church increased its activities and its number of adherents. In 1874, John Horden's translation of hymns into Cree syllabics was published, and by 1882, John Rae was able to write the following about the Cree in the *London Society of Arts Journal*:

> These Indians during their stay at Moose, met every morning and evening in a large tent, where one of their number read or spoke the service they had been taught, in the most exemplary manner and then all joined in singing a hymn in their native tongue. They were at the time, hundreds of miles away from the priest who had worked this good work among them, so that they were in no way coerced by his personal control. (Rae 1882, 488)

The missionaries did get results, and one man in particular, Reverend W. G. Walton, effected rapid change in Cree music practice in Chisasibi. He devoted thirty-two years (1892–1924) to the people of this parish, extending his efforts into the Natives' daily lives. Reverend Walton learned the Cree language, which enabled him to visit the people regularly and to help resolve conflicts. Just as influential was his provision of material aid whenever it was possible. He adhered strictly to Christian doctrine, made few concessions to traditional Cree belief, and strongly discouraged the drumming and singing associated with Cree spiritual practices.

How did the Cree react to the efforts of this powerful man, who reached to the very foundation of their lives, and attempted change? There is no sure way to know, but some clues include the frequent references to Reverend Walton made by elders in their interviews with me, showing that Reverend Walton has become a legendary figure in Chisasibi. One elder said: "Reverend Walton taught the people" (Martinhunter 1982). Another said, "I remember Reverend Walton and the minister before him. We called him 'grandfather'" (Pepabano 1982). The qualities now attributed to Reverend Walton match those traditionally valued in Indian leaders, such as the ability to see into the future, often through dreaming. Some elders use as evidence for this his prediction that white people would come to Chisasibi and that many things would change. In addition, according to Hyman (1971, 35), Reverend Walton is today seen as strong, *sabio*, in the traditional Cree sense of the word. *Sabio* means that he had no boss, for he did not let the Anglican church superiors dictate to him, and that he could make people go to church not by force but by rhetorical persuasion, a quality valued by the Cree. Thus, Reverend Walton is perceived now as a great man because he possessed the very qualities the Cree traditionally valued. He had, and continues to have, influence over them. In the 1980s, the elders I met remembered him in their conversations, and still observed his imposed taboos concerning the drum and the shaking-tent ceremony.

Christian missionaries such as Reverend Walton understood, if imperfectly, that oral tradition contained all of the Cree history and belief. The priests learned to speak Cree, and immediately translated the English hymns, using Evan's syllabics, into the Algonquian language. At the same time, as mentioned above, they discouraged the traditional drumming which they knew to be fundamental to Cree ritual practice. In northern Manitoba, elder Matt Sinclair described the consequences of the arrival of priests as follows:

> It was just shortly later that the priest first came to Pukatawagan and they heard about it in Granville. The priest had the first mass out on the island in Pukatawagan Lake. After it was over, the priest made everybody throw their drums into the water. (Brightman 2002, 162)

Thus, much traditional musical practice, in both Manitoba and Quebec, has ceased, particularly in the more public ceremonies that were replaced by Christian rites. The drums, though, live on in memory, and I have heard stories about drums, carefully wrapped and sealed with pitch, waiting for the right time to be pulled from lake bottoms.

As Christian thought was taking hold of the Cree, so was their reliance upon trapping and trading for a livelihood. But as Adrian Tanner has observed regarding the Mistassini Cree, the people adopted a two-part life defined not only by mode of production, but also by ideology (Tanner 1979). Many Cree worked at the Chisasibi settlement, and most others spent at least some time there each year. While they were in the settlement, the Cree performed the rites of Christianity and sang the Christian hymns. When they returned to the bush each fall for trapping and subsistence hunting, they resumed much of their traditional mental life, repeating the myths and rituals associated with the hunt, and singing the old songs which helped to ensure its success. Frank Speck described a similar duality of life for the Montagnais and the Naskapi, neighbours of the Cree: "When the hunters have returned to the interior, they are again under the thrall of the spiritual forces of the forest" (Speck 1935, 30).

Fiddle Music

While working at the trading post, the Cree would have heard the fiddles, and probably the bagpipes, of the Hudson's Bay Company men, especially those from the Scottish Orkney Islands. By the last half of the eighteenth century, many company servants were of mixed Cree/European origin. In addition to their names, such as Beardy and Flett, the Scots brought their fiddles and fiddle tunes. Fiddle music presented a new "language" of exchange readily acquired by the Cree through face-to-face transmission of cultural knowledge. The music transcended the boundaries of spoken language and culture; indeed, it was a seamless fit, requiring little or no change in the beliefs and language that underpinned the Natives' subsistence lifestyle. One elder told me that they sometimes used fiddles instead of drums to accompany their hunting songs.

The fiddle tunes did require musical changes to fit the Cree sound ideal, with its steady rhythm phrased not by metres and silences but endless word and syllable patterns. But as products of oral tradition, they were easily changed by the Cree. Cree fiddling is unique, and I believe that their variety of styles, and the freedom they express in altering the tunes, is truly the wellspring of music creation. The Cree introduced so much innovation to fiddling and fiddling tunes that one could say they created a new genre of music.[5] Each fiddler has his own version of the tunes, which they change between and even during performances. The fiddle was a new voice but followed the same music traditions as the hunters' songs: an individual performer who made small alterations in the tunes on each repetition. The musical uniformity required by group music-making did not begin until the 1950s with the advent of country music bands consisting of drums, fiddles, guitars, and basses.

Scots fiddling is characterized by regular metres such as the three-beat waltzes or four-beat reels, in contrast to Native fiddling, which does not obey these metrical divisions, although it does have a strong one-beat pulse. Furthermore, Scots fiddle tunes are structured into regular divisions of thirty-two bars, which are subdivided into four-bar phrases. Cree tunes are different: they add beats, especially at cadences (the concluding notes), they subtract beats by overlapping phrases; and they like to elaborate the first phrase of the melody. This often results in phrases of three or five beats, instead of the Scottish four. And there may be three or five complete phrases within a section of the tune, rather than the four of Scots fiddling. Anne Lederman has noted similar changes made by the Ojibwe (1987, 8–13).

The fiddling tradition in Quebec continues. In the community of Wemindji (Paint Hills), which has a population of approximately six hundred, I met at least seven men who played fiddle, and several others who accompanied them on guitar. In 1984, while recording the hunting songs of the James Bay Cree, I couldn't help but hear, and finally record, an evening of fiddling with two fiddlers. The percussive sound of the musicians' foot-tapping made the little house vibrate so vigorously that I had to cradle the microphone in a pillow for recording.

Of the nineteen fiddle tunes I recorded in Wemindji, twelve remain unnamed by the Cree. All are likely of Scottish origin. A southern fiddler was able to identify seven of the fiddle tunes as follows: "Old Joe Clark" (two versions), "Soldiers Joy" (two versions), "Boil the Cabbage Down," "Fisher's Hornpipe," "Devil's Dream," "Rubber Dolly," and "Mississippi Sawyer." Figure 2.1 is a transcription of the popular tune "Soldiers Joy," to which I have added the foot sounds. In this rendition the metre is regular.

Old-time Cree fiddlers use short bow strokes, one note per stroke, which gives the music a strong percussive sound. Some believe that the vigorous foot-tapping takes the place of a drumbeat.

In these ways, the Cree altered the received music and dance to fit their existing sound ideal. The fiddle, like the Christian hymnary, was among the few ideational objects of European origin to be immediately adopted by the Cree. Fiddling was congruent with existing ways of cultural learning, and the portable instrument could be carried easily to the hunting camps. Fiddle tunes were learned by listening and watching. Children were not overtly taught; in fact, one well-known fiddler who learned by observing

Figure 2.1: "Soldiers Joy" fiddle tune (Roderick and Bobby Georgekish, Wemindji, 1984)

his father and uncles said the only time he could play was when his parents left the house. Fiddles were costly and not readily obtainable, but they could be ordered from the Eaton's catalogue or the Hudson's Bay Company. Some fiddlers made their own. The Inuit fashioned stringed instruments from tin cans.

By the end of the twentieth century, the fiddling tradition in northern Manitoba was close to moribund, and many fiddles sat idle in their cases. This situation changed dramatically when Frontier School Division, headquartered in Winnipeg, Manitoba, introduced fiddle classes in selected northern schools. By 2004, the division employed eight instructors, reached twenty communities, and had approximately one thousand enthusiastic young musicians learning to fiddle. Today, many more potential students await teachers, and hopefully they will be trained by the generation now learning to fiddle. The training, often provided by southerners, emphasizes notation and ear skills equally, so the tunes do not have the rhythmic flexibility of the earlier Cree style, but they are providing a much-needed musical outlet and sense of cultural continuity for the youths in the isolated communities.

Dances

Like the tunes, the dances done to fiddle music were an amalgam of Native and non-Native. They combined the British square patterns with the traditional Indian steps. There was no caller; dancers knew what to do. In Manitoba, an elder told me of two dances, one named after the rabbit, the other after a scarf. The rabbit dance usually involved four couples, with each man dancing as if chasing a rabbit, represented by his female partner. The scarf dance can be compared to the Scottish sword dance, in which swords are placed on the ground to form a cross. The scarf dance began with the men using a scarf to catch a partner. This dance was referred to as the *Ta pi ska kan ni si mo win*, in which a scarf was looped around the woman's head and held by her partner. The partners then moved around a circle of the other dancers. Scarves would then be placed on the ground in the shape of a cross, and the male dancer would do a jig without touching the scarves. At the end of this jig, the dancer would catch the ends of the scarves with his feet and pull them into a pile. He could not touch the scarf with his hands, nor stop dancing until his jig was complete. The dancers performed one at a time, competing with one another.

Music and Education

Formal education must be considered in discussing the music history of the Cree. Before the Second World War, the Anglican mission gave primary-grade schooling to coastal bands in Chisasibi, and in 1933 they were authorized by the Department of Indian Affairs to operate a residential school. Scant mention is made of music by the graduates of residential schools, and likewise in the spate of studies about these schools. Author Agnes Grant (2004) believes the direct effect of residential school education on Native song was small indeed. In *Shingwauk's Vision: A History of Native Residential Schools*, the historian J. R. Miller mentions brass bands, a dance around the maypole, the game Ring Around the Rosey, and a few other isolated instances of music, and does finally conclude that "former teachers and students agree unanimously that music and sports were the saving features of residential school experience" (1996, 179). Even if this European music was seen as a good feature of the schools, however, it does show that the youngsters were kept distant from their own song tradition.

The school in Chisasibi came under federal control in 1952, but the use of the English language and the culturally unsuitable text materials caused the students to lag years behind their peers farther south. In 1972, the first regional high school, established at Chisasibi, was plagued by the homesickness of the students and the high cost of boarding them away from home. Although enrollment grew, so did dropouts and a feeling of alienation from the school programs. In contrast to the print materials developed by the earlier missionaries, the school materials were not relevant to the students in language or in content. Moreover, the mostly young teachers from the south were frequently uninformed about the local culture. In their role as the new "storytellers," they were insensitive to the needs of their audience. For example, in one northern community I asked children what songs they knew. Of the seven songs named, three were Christian ("Silent Night," "Mine, Mine, Mine," "I Have a Jubilee Down in My Heart") and the remaining four were "I'm Taking Home a Baby Bumblebee," "They Say that in the Army," "Popcorn, Chewing Gum, Peanuts and Bubblegum," and "Ten Little Indians"! To remedy this situation, efforts have been made to train local people to research their history and language, and to turn this information into teaching materials. One of these projects was actually under way as early as 1969. This "Creeways" project was assisted by John and Gertie Murdoch and McMaster University anthropologists under Richard Preston. These sorts of efforts continue across Canada's north, as does the training of Cree teachers.

Music and the Media

An extremely significant medium for changing Cree music in the isolated settlements was the reception of commercial American radio. As I just mentioned, most print remained irrelevant to Algonquian speakers, but country songs, even in English, like the fiddle tunes before them, held and continue to hold immediate appeal. Bill C. Malone observed in 1975 that, in the United States, "the phenomenon that has exerted the most profound urbanizing influence upon rural areas is the radio" (34). This applies as well to northern Canada after the installation of high-powered radio transmitters in the 1930s. The Canadian Broadcasting Service (CBC), formed in 1958, has always received scant attention from northerners, but its offspring such as Native Communications Incorporated (NCI) are now central to community musical life.

The next significant change for the Cree was the beginning of Anik satellite broadcast television in the 1970s. Television had immediate enormous appeal. In 1979, I witnessed an entire room filled with northerners trying to watch the one available television set broadcasting southern shows entirely in English. The Aboriginal People's Television Network (APTN), established in 1999, permits the Cree to hear the music of their neighbours, but language barriers remain firm. A Cree person is not going to understand or copy a song in the Inuktitut or Athabascan languages.

Other means of communication have advanced steadily into Cree lands. Air service from the south to Chisasibi began in 1932. Across northern Canada there are daily flights into a majority of northern communities; there are all-weather roads and more planned, and direct-dial telephone service. Two generations of Cree have grown up conversing in English and enjoying North American popular culture. Few living persons speak only Cree.

The cumbersome radios of the 1930s were at the beginning of a rapidly spreading communications revolution. No matter how remote the community, by the 1990s there were televisions in every home, and fax machines and computer modems in every office, across northern Canada. Teenagers and trappers alike now wear portable audio equipment, and the cornucopia of musics available represents a huge change from a society in which one heard only the songs of one's grandparents.

At the beginning of the twenty-first century, the sharing of physical space is less and less necessary for groups defined by cultural commonalities. For example, the music tastes of some Norway House dwellers may have more in common with city people in Winnipeg than with those on a neighbouring reserve such as Oxford House. The pre-media world of small human groupings bound together by oral traditions has given way to the various groupings made possible by the media, even on reserves physically separated from the majority of Canadians. In a later chapter, we shall see how rapid change has, for many Cree, caused a crisis of confidence in ancestral ways and led to a loss of local musical culture. However, in this century, Aboriginals have become part of the world musical community, and some look to distant Aboriginal traditions such as powwow song to renew a sense of local Native identity.

In view of the tremendous pressure on northern Cree culture, the continued existence of the old songs to the end of the twentieth century is, in some respects, remarkable. Anthropologist Harvey Feit reiterates this observation at the societal level:

> Hunting and gathering societies have continued to exist in the northern parts of Canada despite 150 to 350 years of involvement with the international fur-trade, despite 25 to 75 years of administrative involvement with national and provincial governmental structures, and despite governmental policies that have frequently been based on the assumption that hunting was a dying way of life. (1982, 376)

3

Song and Survival

Imagine growing up on a northern reserve at the turn of the twentieth century. You do not see solid old buildings, iron fences, or monuments to past heroes. No sweeping changes are forecast for your village—no new factories or housing developments—just the forest, rivers, and animals that renew themselves in the same fashion year after year.

Your family does not write personal memoirs, keep photograph albums, or even keep strict watch over its personal belongings, but your relatives do tell and retell the oral narratives that help you to know your origins and ancestors.

On a winter night, you and your family talk quietly, sitting on the fragrant pine boughs covering the ground. All eyes are fixed on the fire in the centre of the migiwap (tent). Your grandparents, mother and father, two sisters, and the adopted son of a deceased friend are satisfied and warm after a meal of roast bear meat, powdered fish preserved in goose oil, freshly baked bannock, and warm tea. At this time, your grandfather, reclining on his side, picks up a drum beater made from a sturdy stick wound with tanned hide. He begins to beat softly on the drum hung by a leather cord from a pole of the migiwap.

Tonight is joyous because a bear has been killed. The old hunter's voice merges with the loud vibrations of the drum, and the buzzing sound of the fetal caribou bones stretched across the open side of the drum never fails to give you a shiver of delight. You understand few of the words in the song, but you know that your grandfather is thanking the bear for giving himself to the family. Before singing again, your grandfather says the following:

Song 14
I'm going to sing about the bear
About the man who lives with a bear
And follows the bear around

The bear lives off berries
The man asks the bear for berries
It's about the man and the bear (Pepabano 1982)

In this chapter, we read about the hunting songs, their meaning, and their music as described by the six James Bay Cree elders profiled earlier. To understand the hunting songs, one must remember that obtaining enough food was a constant challenge for the Cree. Despite the large populations of each animal species in the north, there is low species diversity, and the populations are subject to extreme fluctuation. This affects their predators, both human and animal. For example, once each decade the rabbit population will almost vanish, causing severe depopulation of the lynx and making times tough for humans too. While not a major food source of the Cree, the rabbit fills in when large game is not captured. Elders recall how, before government transfer payments, people experienced periods of privation, even starvation:

> Here is another incident I remember from when I was very young.
> There were five families living with us in the bush at that time.
> They only had two small ptarmigans.
> That's to give you an example of how food was very scarce. (Robert Bearskin 1982)

To find, capture, and consume their prey, Cree hunters traditionally used all their physical and sensory abilities. Knowledge of hunting tools and hunting practices was important too, in order to make best use of the snares, deadfalls, bow and arrow, crossbow, spear, bird bola, and fishing nets. Traditionally, food storage was not widely practised because of the difficulty of transporting meat (usually smoked so as to be lighter) and of travelling to distant caches; moreover, the Cree preferred fresh meat (Brightman 2002, 360). The preferred strategy for most kinds of food used to be to follow the animals. Robert Blackned of Chisasibi described both strategies to me:

> In those days, a lot of people went deep inland
> They moved camp regularly
> When the snow began to melt in the spring
> We would go to a different camp again
> This would be our fish camp
> Where we know the fish would be plenty

We wouldn't waste any of the fish
We would smoke it, dry it, save it for future use.
Some of the smoked fish would be left there
If you came back during the summer
You would find your fish in good condition (Blackned 1984)

Although physical strength and exertion is necessary, capturing a wild animal also requires knowledge, thought, and fortitude. Allied to these characteristics are ideational strategies such as knowing the metaphysical basis for hunting, and remembering and sharing the knowledge by means of oral tradition. The songs formed part of this oral narrative; they contained information about the animals, the local environment, and hunting practices. More importantly, they energized the hunter, both mentally and physically, helping him to "see" the animals. They can be thought of as an important part of the whole hunting strategy. According to Richard Preston, "In an essentially mental or spiritual way, the songs influence the animals, making the hunt more successful" (2002, 199).

Song as a survival tactic is a difficult concept for non-Natives to comprehend. In western society, most view song as entertainment. We can understand Cree hunting songs better by thinking of them as what anthropologists call "traditional ecological knowledge," like making a rabbit snare or "chiselling" the beaver (tapping to locate their passages). The hunting songs fulfill most definitions of traditional ecological knowledge: they are a holistic way of knowing, specific to a place and to a people, and generally different in form from other types of knowledge such as that acquired in institutions. The information contained in a song is learned from experience or from family and community through oral narratives. They show how things work, and offer an immediate guide to action. Such songs are found among all peoples who gain their primary needs directly from nature. In recent years, First Nations traditional ecological knowledge (TEK) has been officially recognized in government policy, especially in northern Canada, and incorporated into the processes of environmental assessment and resource management.

As I mentioned in the Introduction, the six aged East Cree hunters who shared their songs with me spoke only Cree, and were able to live relatively undisturbed on their ancestral lands until the 1970s. By the 1980s, only one of them was still actively hunting, so my discussions with them were mostly of reminiscences. They enjoyed singing and talking about their songs, and indeed were eager to share their knowledge because they feared that their way of life was over.

Long ago Indians knew various ways and means
To survive on the land
That's what I mainly sang about—my experience on the land.
The people mainly sang about hunting
The animals they hunted, the water, the rapids, the land
While they worked, like making snowshoes
The songs were about whatever they were doing.
Nowadays I don't think the young people do that
They don't sing while they are out hunting or working. (Lameboy 1982)

The hunting songs (*niitooh-nikamon*) are a personal expression of emotion, yet not one of the eighty-six that I recorded expressed sadness or regret. In *Cree Narrative*, Richard Preston observed that "expressions of hope are usually in the form of songs" (1975, 194). The hunter William Jack said, "I sing when I'm happy" (1982). The songs predicted successful outcomes for an occupation that is challenging and exciting in the extreme. The vivid images in the songs show the hunter's appreciation of the animals and all of nature.

Songs provided facts about the animals and the local environment; they contained ancient wisdom, yet were readily changed to deal with new situations; they were prayers, aiding communication with the spirit beings of the animals and thereby ensuring animals for the hunt; they energized the hunter and, at the same time, their frequent humour must have made bearable the uncertainty of capturing wild animals; they were mental play, bringing disparate subjects together, as well as artistic creations. Although the words are often tantalizingly obscured, their meaning is not secret. The hunters took great care to explain the songs. This cumulative knowledge, arrived at through shared experiences and validated over long periods of time and across wide areas, renders the songs and stories authoritative. They are part of the framework of communal activity. Moreover, hunting songs provide a heuristic example of biologist Edward O. Wilson's concept of consilience (1999), the essential unity of the arts and sciences, even of nature and nurture. All westerners recognize song as art—songs are learned and patterned cultural behaviour. But to the Cree, they are not just artistic objects, they are a technology. Cree use of song suggests that the predisposition to create song, like language, is rooted deeply in human genetic inheritance. Despite the severity of the Subarctic and the considerable physical energy required to drum and sing, hunters chose songs as an essential part of the hunt.

It is not enough, however, to think of the songs simply as storehouses of local information or scientific knowledge. The performance of a song stimulated the intuition and the creative power needed to capture a wild animal. Beyond this, and most importantly for the Cree hunters, the songs also allowed the hunter's spirit to communicate with the spirits of the animals.

Communication with Animals

As the scholar Richard Preston remarks, "The Cree attribute human qualities to animals, such as logical thought, dreams, and emotions" (2002, 203). These qualities appear in the characters of the animals as represented in dreams, and in songs that link images in the dream world to animals in the real world. Referring to animals, Speck wrote, "Their equality is spiritual, which eclipses the physical" (1935, 76). The songs not only give information about the animal but also serve as an inspiration for human action:

I'm going to sing about the winterbird
I was thinking as I was walking with my snowshoes
I was thinking, I wish I could fly
Then I suddenly remembered the winterbird
He was very fast with his snowshoes
He was so fast that I thought I was flying like a winterbird
Then I thought I would steal the song of the winterbird. (Jack 1982)

The words of the songs depict human and animal exchanges, even conversations. Consider the following song, sung by Samson Lameboy:

Song 52
We used to kill geese in the fall and in the spring.
Every time I saw the geese I felt I could communicate with them
And they could communicate with me
They would sing, "I don't think you can outdo me."
The geese were saying that, sort of challenging one another
The geese would challenge him
This song is about the bird challenging me.

Another hunter, Robert Potts, sung about a fox speaking to him:

Song 29
When I went out trapping, to check the traps, sometimes there was a fox. When I approached, the fox seemed to say, "Here's your trap," and raised it up as if he was going to give it to me. The fox seemed to say, "Is this your trap?" (Potts 1982)

One of the animals commonly spoken to by hunters is the bear. To the Cree, the bear resembles humans more than any other species: it can walk on its hind legs, and will eat humans, just as humans eat it. The bear is seen as the most spiritually powerful animal and is addressed as *Nimosin*, "my father." Brightman (2002, 146) cites another name used by the Rock Cree, *apitawioiniw*, meaning "half-human." In George Pepabano's song below, the man is asking the bear to share:

Song 14
I'm going to sing about the bear
It's about this man who lives with a bear
The bear lives off berries
The man asks the bear for some berries
It's about the man and the bear (Pepabano 1982)

The image of the berries here is an interesting symbol. It could represent the bear's life. It could also allude to beads, the traditional name for which was "spirit berries" (Speck 1935, 192), and which were a symbolic food given to husbands by their wives. In any case, the image is clearly used to show a bond between human and animal.

Chipeeyoo is a beaver who sometimes appears in human form. Such bonds are a common theme in the hunting songs, and may even be depicted as a marriage:

Song 42
I used to dream about Chipeeyoo
Chipeeyoo was supposed to marry this man
She didn't listen, she could hardly wait to get to the river
Not too long after, Chipeyoo married the man
He had a brother in Rupert House
The brother wanted to kill him through supernatural powers.
The brother came this way, to the place called "wadash"
You know how hard it is to get to, just along the shore here
They went as far as Great Whale River and that's where Chipeeyoo's
    husband died
So one time the brother went and checked out a beaver dam
He went and looked inside the dam
And guess who was laying there, Chipeeyoo!
And the brother said to Chipeeyoo
"Why didn't you tell me that I killed your man?"
He was a difficult animal to hunt, the beaver. (Martinhunter 1982)

The discussion of the goose dance ceremony and healing plants in chapter 1 showed the traditional Cree belief in a supreme spirit being inherent in each animal and plant. These spirit beings serve to remind the individual of the existence of something greater than himself, something immortal. Improper treatment of an animal communicates disrespect to the animal spirit. In *Grateful Prey*, Robert Brightman cites examples of the Cree desire for the animals to die with minimal pain. Prolonged suffering is believed to make the meat taste bad and to diminish the success of future hunting (2002, 110–11). George Snowboy told me how such suffering was a cause for concern:

> Later on in the evening I decided to go to sleep
> I couldn't find the fox that I had wounded
> I worried about him because I thought that he would be in pain. (1982)

Before singing his song about the bird, Abraham Martinhunter described a similar concern:

Introduction to Song 43
I came to the first rapids and I saw a little bird near the rapids
Then my oldest son was going to take a shot at the little bird
I told him "don't." (1982)

Despite this respect for animal spirits, the smaller food animals were sometimes the subject of the hunter's jokes, particularly regarding physical characteristics. For example, when I asked William Jack to sing a porcupine song, he replied, "Oh no, that would hurt too much." William's song about the rabbit (see Appendix II, Song 5) tells about rubbing rabbit entrails on moose sinew that was then used for snaring the rabbit, a process that also offered humour:

> We used to say we laugh at the rabbit[1]
> Because he's going to eat his own insides.

William sang a very short song about a small lake trout, then, chuckling, said, "That's it! A very short song" (see Appendix II, Song 4). He also described his song about the seagulls (Song 6) as funny, saying:

> I was a guide with my son who speaks English. The white men always had tape recorders and wanted me to sing or tell stories. And I saw this seagull flying along searching for food. Then I said to my son, "They always make me sing songs or tell stories. Here's the song I'm going to tell him because white people eat seagulls:
> > The seagull, the seagull, the seagull
> > That eats and eats and eats the whiteman
> > That's the one who always eats the whiteman."

The translator of this song, Violet Bates, explained it thus: "We Natives don't eat seagulls—they're junk eaters. William Jack turned the song around—instead of singing the whiteman ate the seagull, he sang the seagull ate the whiteman. Like many of the songs the Native people sing, they turn them around" (1982).

To the Cree hunters, dreams were an important source of knowledge and motivation. Interestingly, scientists are again investigating this as a serious topic for research. Neuropsychologist Mark Solms views dreams as a primary emotional mechanism that energizes most goal-directed interactions, similar to Freud's libido (2004, 82–89). The Cree dream songs provide support for Solm's hypothesis, and for the wish-fulfillment theory of dreams. Abraham Martinhunter (1982) sang about a dream that prefigured a real event:

Song 40
I was dreaming one night
And I saw two foxes running around
One was dark and one was light
Then I went out to hunt in my canoe and I killed fifteen fox.

In the songs and dreams, the animals, even though they must be killed, are loved as the source of life. They are not the target of aggression. Abraham gave an example of this:

Song 41
You know how it is when a man falls in love with a girl
He holds the girl
You know those two religious women
I dreamed that both of them were on either side of me
One of the other religious women couldn't come near me.
When I awoke from my dream I had trapped two otter
There were supposed to be three otter but one got away
And couldn't come near to my traps.
That's how I am singing about the otter.

In the song, the real-life otters are associated with figures of love and respect in the dream. Incidentally, animals do not appear in the dream-world only as characters. They too create dreams that may have an impact on a hunter's success.

I told my father that I was going to make a net for the beaver
And he left
While he was gone I made the net
My father came back and asked what I was doing
My father said, "You are not supposed to make the net during the day, but
    at night
During the day the beaver is sleeping
And at night the beaver comes out
The beaver is going to dream about your net
Because he sleeps during the day." (Hughboy 1982)

Some of the dream songs are personal and endure a lifetime. The hunter, when a youth, would dream of a particular animal, perhaps a caribou. From then on, the caribou song would become part of his hunting ritual. After he died, other singers would sing his caribou song. Samson Lameboy said: "Each person had their own different song—what they want to have—the animal. That's what they sang about, even a little boy" (1982). These dream songs (*anikamotahnibat*) would continue to appear throughout one's life. They were once highly valued as a source of knowledge and power.[2]

Knowledge and Power in Songs

Because of the cyclical nature of subarctic animal populations, the knowledge of older individuals, such as the knowledge contained in their songs, was invaluable. While growing up, most Cree lived through times of scarcity. Periodic shortages were anticipated, not in fear, but by choosing appropriate strategies. One strategy for the experienced hunter was to "see" a desired animal in visions and to bring that animal closer through songs. Success in hunting came with the singing of a powerful song (*abamichimat*). Edward Ottereyes said, "People sang a lot to protect their hunting" (1982). Drumming was implied in the songs even when the drums themselves were not used. Kenneth S. Lane (1863, 36), writing about the Cree's neighbours, the Montagnais, from 1600–40, observed that during a famine the people would stay in their cabins and drum and sing continually as a means to obtain food. Moreover, they believed the songs indirectly helped the hunt by changing the weather. William Jack described an instance of this: "They made the songs up from the event they wanted to happen" (1982).

Some hunters were particularly adept at communicating with the spirit beings for the procurement of food. It was recognized that some hunters had more powerful songs. One Cree man said to me, "The best singers were the best hunters." The hunters have many stories of those who have attained power through dreams and song. William Jack told of a man named Jimmy Redeyes, feared by the people. He was asked to sing and make the wind turn around so the geese could fly. William said, "I heard him sing two goose songs. He just sang, didn't use drums. In the morning the wind had turned around. The north wind had become warm south winds." This is his description of the song:

Song 60
I'm going to sing you a song made by Jimmy Redeyes
He had very special powers
He was a very powerful man, but I wasn't afraid of him

I still wrestled him
I'm going to sing one of Jimmy's songs that he sang
When he made the wind turn around
I'm going to sing about what Jimmy looked like
And the song is going to go towards a goose song.

William continued with a story about a thaumaturgic act that involved song. He explained that wooden poles in the water are sometimes mistaken for fish; in this song, however, William's grandfather used his singing to transform some wood into fish:

Song 58

One time my grandfather was in the bush
They couldn't get anything; they were near starvation
There were a lot of kids around
So my grandfather asked his wife to cut down some wood
Four pieces of wood that were longer than normal size.
My grandmother said,
"I wonder what he is going to do with those four pieces?"
The old man said, "Bring the cloth here that you use to clean the meat"
They brought a canvas cloth and laid it over the four logs
He put a canvas cloth over them too and started singing.

Now let us look at the hunter's description of his songs for signs of empirical knowledge of the physical world. Most of the songs I recorded focus on animals. Several consider other aspects of nature, but they are invariably "turned" to include an animal, as in the following:

Song 28

This song is about a low cloud; there is a name for every cloud.
There were times when I did kill lots of geese
Just like clouds moving fast.
How fast the clouds go by when it's really cloudy. (Potts 1982)

The song description below emphasizes the ideal animal, the healthy animal:

Song 2

I used to love going fox hunting
I saw a fox very well built, a healthy fox
He was orange; he had an orange-brown back. (Jack 1982)

Songs can inform us about animal habits:

Song 3

I sing about how the beaver keeps his food underwater
How the trees float down the water because of the beaver. (Jack 1982)

Song 38

This song is about the goose
He's going to fly differently in the fall from the way he flies in the spring
This bird doesn't fool around, he means business. (Martinhunter 1982)

Weather affects the timing of the migration of the geese:

Song 78

I used to sing this song in the bush and at home too
This spring was early; it was hot early
The geese flew to their northern breeding grounds
So the people didn't kill many. (Rupert 1982)

The hunters sang about specific technologies for the hunt:

Song 18

This is a song that my father used to sing
When he went in his canoe to look for geese.
He made the canoe and he was very skilful in making the canoe
Out of birchbark and the roots from the tree. (Pepabano 1982)

Song 21

This is a toboggan song, how it is used for travelling
This was the only way we travelled a long time ago
This song tells a story with pictures, you could almost see them
I learned this song from my father and taught it to my elder sons
When we were trapping in the fall
We sing about each way of travelling—canoe or toboggan. (Pepabano 1982)

Song 53

That's how the Indians were; they could hunt all kinds of animals
They could hunt under the ice for fish
And use a spear to dig a hole in the ground
And throw in a string or a hook to the other side of the hole to make a net
That's how they feed their families on the land
I'm going to sing about a tool for fishing under the ice in wintertime. (Lameboy 1982)

Song 67

I'm going to sing about the goose
And how they used to preserve the geese in wooden barrels,
Those first barrels.
This song is about when you first start hunting in the morning.
When you're sitting in the blind waiting for them to come.
This is my own song. (Martinhunter 1982)

Song 69
This is a song while I was still trapping fox.
In the song I sang about the bait and also about the measuring stick.
I'm singing about the white fox; I used to kill a lot.
You don't see white foxes anymore, they're extinct. (Martinhunter 1982)

We can also learn about hunting practices:

Song 31
This is a song about the beaver. It dives in the winter into a hole in the ice. I used to follow the sound underneath the ice. Now he reaches his point (of view) where he could come up. Usually when I finished blocking his way out, that's where they all were, nine in the family. My song, "My ice-chisel is following it," is my own. I sang it when following the beaver. (Potts 1982)

Song 71
This is the beaver's plate song. We call it that, because it's a trap. The beaver, that's the food, as if he's setting his plate. The song is about a beaver; I'm trying to trick them. I start from the beaver's den—all the way along to the door; it's like a bottle. You make a noise like hitting a bottle. The beaver hears that and it comes. Lots of times I caught beaver like that. (Pepabano 1982)

Song 63
Fish sometimes change the area where they feed, so you have to move to another area. (Lameboy 1984)

The following is the only reference in the songs to making medicine. It includes a reference to an organ, but the translator was not sure which one. It may be the castor gland of the beaver. (One hunter told me that he rubbed the thick brown odiferous secretion from this onto his dog's nose, so as to make it good at hunting.)

Song 42
The man used to tell her to hook all the *bootsinaw* and hang them sideways
Bootsinaw is a part of the beaver they used for medicine; they were dried on a small stick. (Martinhunter 1982)

The hunter sang often to himself upon first awakening to welcome the new day and to strengthen his personal power for the day's hunt. Only in a few circumstances, such as when waiting for geese in a blind or when setting traps, could the hunter actually sing while hunting. Much of the time he had to remain as silent as possible. He would usually sing again for his own pleasure at the end of the day, while resting in the *migiwap*, as a celebration of the day's work. Introducing one of his songs, Robert Potts said:

> When I was a young man, I would walk a long way when hunting, but I never got tired. I walked hard to find food for my family. I made the song up a long time ago. I look forward to going even farther when hunting and sing to keep my spirits up.

The song tradition is rooted in the practice of generations. The hunter's father was an important source of his songs. Men sometimes sang songs composed by women, and would readily acknowledge this when introducing the song, as in the following examples:

> **Song 18 (Pepabano):** This is a song my father used to sing when he went in his canoe to look for geese.
> **Song 20:** I'm going to sing the song of the inlanders, the people from the east.
> **Song 21:** The songs that I sang, I picked up from my father and my grandfather, generation to generation.
> **Song 33 (Potts):** The men used to sing this song.
> **Song 35:** I used to hear someone singing this, it's not my song.
> **Song 45 (Martinhunter):** This is my father's song about the rapids.
> **Song 67:** This is my own song.
> **Song 73 (Pepabano):** This song has been passed down from generation to generation.

The songs range in age from ancient to improvised for the occasion, as Edward Ottereyes mentioned: "[The singers] don't think up the song ahead of time, they just sing what comes to mind." Some of the songs are delightfully topical and show adaptation to new circumstances. For example, the hunters created songs that sounded like a hunting song but incorporated the "news," such as the effects of George Spence's whisky:

Song 47
The waves were huge.
I had some whisky and I wasn't afraid of anything
We used to be in the ship
That old man by the name of George Spence
Used to give us some whisky
The waves against the ship were huge
It used to make the white man frantic
Then we used to drink some whisky and we became brave. (Martinhunter 1982)

Some of the old songs show the adoption of Christian concepts. This song refers both to Christian ideas (our Father) and a traditional reverence for the morning just at daybreak:

Song 56
It's so beautiful when the sun comes out early in the morning
How beautiful He made it (repeated)
How beautiful He made the sky, our Father
Our Father who made the sky
How beautiful He made it. (Lameboy 1984)

The hunter's toolkit was highly specialized. This was evident in their vast vocabulary of hunting and trapping terms. To be effective hunting tools, songs had to be carefully allocated, precisely timed, and rendered as well as possible to fit the Cree sound ideal. They also had to be sung by appropriate people in correct circumstances. For example, the men stated that women never sang the hunting songs, nor did they drum. William Jack said, "You never saw women using the drum; it was always the men." Robert Potts told me: "Women do not do serious singing, only for their children." This is likely the result of taboos. Women have traditionally been the subject of several Cree taboos—for example, a woman must never step over a fishnet that is spread out for repair, for fear of endangering the catch; the life-giving strength of female fertility, particularly during menstruation, could cause animals to escape death, and interfere with the regeneration of animal souls in fetal or mature forms. However, a few older women *did* sing hunting songs, indicating that their age and lack of fertility meant that they no longer threatened hunting success.

Women's Songs

Cree women did have songs for their own tasks: sewing; making *babiche* for snowshoes; setting snares, traps, and nets; cutting wood; making the fire; and preparing food.

Song 54
When the hunter left, the woman would leave at the same time
To get logs for the home, that was her job to get firewood
The women, their place was in the home
This was one song they had; a woman made up this song.
The woman is singing about getting logs for the family
That's how she cooks for the children
She's singing about getting firewood

A woman sang this song about her wood and it was passed along. (Lameboy 1984)

But just because the women's songs were not directly about hunting didn't mean that they too couldn't influence the hunt. Samson suggests that the acts of cutting wood and singing a woodcutting song would influence a hunt positively:

Song 61
Long ago, men when they were in the bush would be gone as soon as the sun came up. The same with the women; she would be out in the bush cutting wood. She cut wood because she wanted her husband to bring something home for her to cook. So women sang these kinds of songs. It was mostly old women who sang the songs. (Lameboy 1984)

Job Bearskin (1982), husband of Mary, offered another explanation:

She was chopping wood—it was like her hunting. This was one of her favourite chores—getting wood. This is why she made the song like this. She used the wood like this, while men hunted, to cook.

Unfortunately, little has been observed or recorded about the songs women sang, for they are shy about singing for non-family members. After considerable urging by her husband, Job, Mary Bearskin sang two songs:

Song 75
This is one of my grandmother's songs. This is when she was using the tendons, when she was working with her grandmother.

Song 76
This when I was chopping wood. So you'll believe it now that old women sing. When there's lots of wood near the doorway. (1984)

Few women in Chisasibi sing the old songs, but one singing tradition that has persisted is the singing of lullabies (*ahmamahashonaa niwich*).[3] Although men do sing lullabies, they are mostly in the woman's domain (Blacksmith 2003). The Swampy Cree call these songs in English "humming," "sounds," and "no words," and, in Cree, *mamahosowin*. A variation on the lullaby is a soft whistling sound made by blowing air through pursed lips. Children were put to sleep in a swing suspended from beams, called (in Swampy Cree) *may may pah soon*. The songs consisted of repeated syllables such as *ay yey, bee bee,* or *bow bow* (Snowboy, Song 86).

These lullabies are similar to those described by Ellen Smallboy (1853–1941), a Cree woman born in northern Ontario. When interviewed by Regina Flannery in the 1930s, Mrs. Smallboy said the word for cradle or swing was *mempison* and that a lullaby consists of syllables such as *me-me*

sung over and over to a tune. She had another tune she sang as her child
sat in her lap and she looked for lice (1995, 33). These songs continue to
be sung by women in northern Manitoba, as do songs for teething, called
nowaha kipisisa.

Roddy Garrick of Thompson, Manitoba, said that sometimes there were
words telling the baby to be quiet or to go to sleep so that granny could go
to the dance. Later generations who grew up with country and hymn tunes
hummed or sang these new tunes to their babies. For example, in Grand
Rapids, Manitoba, the following hymn, "The Evening Song," was commonly used as a lullaby:

> Jesus Christ my saviour
> Today pray for me
> To sleep good
> To wake up well (good, happy)
> Bad Thoughts (feelings)
> Take away from me
> My soul I give to you
> My heart is yours. (Garrick 1981)

Like the women, children did not sing hunting songs. The old hunters
recalled hearing the songs as they grew up, but said they couldn't understand them. Robert Blackned of Chisasibi described how he learned to be
a hunter, which may reveal how he also learned the songs:

> There was no book telling you how to do this and how to do that
> You would just learn by observing
> This is how I learned to do other things too
> Like making snowshoes, making paddles
> And various hunting equipment
> I learned from observing and practising and doing it myself
> At first the things that I made didn't look very good
> But I kept trying and trying
> And so I learned how to hunt small game
> Then I learned how to hunt big game
> Then I learned how to make the various hunting equipment
> Then I knew that I was able to survive by myself on the land
> I became a skilled hunter, skilled at making equipment
> I've hunted all kinds of animals
> But the only animal I've never killed
> Is the polar bear and the whale. (Blackned, interviewed by author, 1984)

Song, like story, gives the ability to store and transmit information crucial to survival. The songs help to communicate with the supramundane

world, and are, at the same time, a sensory experience. Creation of a song is mentally stimulating and a psychological tonic, for songs optimistically affirm that the animal will be there for the hunter. The hunters indicated an eagerness to verbally communicate as well as sing the knowledge in the songs. Songs, traditional ecological knowledge, do contribute to Cree survival when sung in a particular environmental niche, at the correct time, and by the proper person.

Personal Elements in Song Content

After listening to several Cree songs, most people can recognize the common characteristics; I explore the commonalities further at the end of this chapter. First, however, I want to discuss the *differences* between the individual singers who contributed to my research, and whose songs are recorded on the CD accompanying this text. Each Cree hunter sings with a quite different vocal quality, shapes his melodic phrases in an idiosyncratic way, and sings about the topics that are significant to him. Robert Potts, for example, was the only hunter to sing about a human relative in a song, one that alluded to the dawn and his sister, whom he called "dawn girl" (Song 32).

Truly, Cree hunting songs fit well with the portrayal of the Cree hunter as an individualist. They hunt independently and, if a leader is chosen, it is only for a particular situation, not for the long term. Cree children are expected to learn independently, to be inner-directed. Youths experience their personal search in solitude, and the animal helper and song bestowed upon them are unique to each person and remain so throughout life.

Moreover, the Cree traditionally lived in small family groupings from fall to spring, surviving on large animals, such as moose, caribou, and deer. Only in spring and fall did families come together to harvest geese, fish, pick berries, and to select marriage partners. At this time they participated in the communal dance events, such as the aforementioned goose dance. Eventually Christian rites supplanted Cree public rites, and hymn-singing became the form of music expression for rites of passage such as funerals, weddings, and births. As public forms of expression, the hymns were, and continue to be, sung with uniformity of performance style in contrast to the individuality of the hunters. They show the result of a life led around permanent communities and long-term leaders. In contrast, the hunting songs and stories (which, let us remember, survived widespread cultural change up until the late twentieth century) were personal forms of expression, a matter of solo reflection rather than public performance.

THE WORDS

You have already experienced the content of the songs as described by the singer before singing the song. Let's look now at the song words that under-lie the music, that—in most cases—remain enigmatic. Several of my young translators, and even one of the more senior ones, could not translate the words.

William Jack commented on the difficulty of understanding other hunters' songs:

> This is one of my grandfather's songs. I didn't really catch the words to this song. The younger generation don't understand. It's not only me, when another old person sings I won't understand what he sings about.
>
> At times the older men would get up in the middle of the night and sing their songs. I would try to catch the words and sing their songs. Now there are some Crees that cannot understand. (1982)

Part of the problem arises at the social level, both from generational and occupational differences. The songs' words come from the subsistence lifestyle, and have meaning only to those who participate in hunting. For example, in the Cree language there are many anatomical words for the parts of animals, and a multitude of terms for hunting tools and weapons that the younger generations no longer understand, as in Abraham Mart-inhunter's song quoted earlier in this chapter, which mentioned a beaver part that the translator didn't know—*bootsinaw*.

Then there is the 'idiosong' of the individual and by the polysynthetic nature of Algonquian languages that lends itself to wordplay and density of meaning as in western poetry. One word, even one syllable, can evoke many images, and, as content, can be layered, creating a rich artistic expres-sion. George Fulford cites the example of the syllable "wusk" in the Algon-quian language, used in words as diverse as "bird," "cloud," and "water lily" (2002). This quality of the languages facilitates a unique process in the creation of a song that the Cree hunters call "turning" the song, as we saw earlier in William Jack's song about the seagulls. They fit as much content into a song as possible, and understanding the meaning is highly dependent upon knowing the context of the song subjects. Consider the following:

Song 79: "A goose song about my new gun."

To understand how images of a new gun and geese are woven together, one needs to know that specific guns are used for specific animals.

Song 73: "If the canoe was there it would be like the little ducks."

Little ducks and canoes on the water look alike.

Song 34: "Fixing the canoe is like gathering up white fish in nets."

Fixing a canoe is slow precise work, just like removing fish from a net without tearing it, while sitting in a bobbing canoe.

There are other cultural imperatives to be considered to understand the obscurity of the words. As we have seen, the content of the songs is freely shared, but the lexical units are obscured. Brightman (2002) tells us the important things are unsaid: songs can have a direct effect on the future. In Cree culture it is prudent not to speak the names of the food animals aloud. For example, in William Jack's song about the fox, it is not named, instead the fox is referred to as an "orange-back."

It is believed that the spirit of the animal hears its name if it is spoken aloud. Thus, larger animals such as the bear are spoken about with respect, especially before or after the hunt. The hunter does not announce the number of the animals he has killed and his family doesn't ask. Harry Hughboy (1984) described returning home after the hunt as follows:

> When you kill a bear and when you go home
> You don't tell your family right away
> You keep it a secret until later
> But because in those times everyone was so hungry
> I just told everyone I had killed a bear

Moreover, there is admiration for non-verbal communication in Native society. Animals are considered superior because they do not need to talk to communicate (Anderson and Bone 2003, 104). This cultural imperative is at work during the shaking tent, when all meanings are obscured. Robert Brightman writes, "One naturally wonders ... whether Crees ever conceive themselves as beings possessing covertly the character of the nonhuman animals of waking life" (Brightman 2002, 185). Certainly, their song tends to be stripped of lexical qualities and to project sheer emotion.

Richard Preston reached the following conclusions about the words:

> If some songs "are not really saying something," and so do not have any known lexical content, other songs do have meaningful words. But these meanings may not be generally understood. In translating the tapes of more than seventy songs, Gertie Murdoch was able to understand only one song on a word-for-word basis, although she had no problems with the conversations that accompanied the songs. (2002, 197)

Likewise in my collection: only two of the eighty-six songs recorded were translatable. One of them is Joseph Rupert's "Trout Song" (Song 81).

TROUT SONG

Figure 3.1: "Trout Song," by Joseph Rupert. Written Cree and English words by Brian Craik

The "Trout Song" (fig. 3.1) is an art song in miniature. Like most of the songs I recorded, it is fleeting, and its meaning is esoteric, except for those few who understand the hunting context and special usages of Cree. It does, however, have words that can be translated.

The words and the four different pitches of this memorable tune are inseparable. The song consists of short musical motifs that are repeated as the words are repeated. Overall, the melody is in two distinct parts: the first part, in which the singer talks to the trout; and the second, in which the fish are described. Internally, the form of the song is replete with stylistic devices, particularly the dropping of word endings. Although you may not read Cree, you can see that the first word is abbreviated to *"me ko"* from *"ma-si me ko"* and repeated this way in line three. In another stylistic device, the syllables *"se-ya-ka"* provide a musical ending. This device is found in many of the songs. Most ingenious is the progressive abbreviation of the word-phrase *"my (fish) hook":*

no ci kwa-ci kan
no
  . . .

Likewise, the word *waskamehyaweyna* (one with shiny sides to touch) is
shortened with repetition.

In the final line, the first word incorporates the suffix *"ako"* plus the
same syllables used for stylistic reasons on the first word, speckled trout.
This word then means "he is invited." The last part (*wi ci me yo*) refers to
another fish, and is built on *wicii*, "to accompany." Nowhere is it said that
the trout is being invited to eat another fish, but it is assumed from the context (Craik 2005). The bait is usually a piece of fish or is made to look like
a fish (Craik 2005).

In this song, Joseph Rupert flatters the trout, encouraging it to take his
hook. His entreaties become more and more persuasive as he repeats "Come
and get my fish hook."

Song Presentation

PRESENTATION

The presentation of the music was as subtle as the words. Each hunter had
a distinctive vocal timbre, but overall they sang in relaxed, quiet tones,
almost in their speaking range, which seemed to blend with the low sound
levels of the northern terrain. It is a world of nuances rather than vivid
colours; even the flowers are miniature. I never heard an attempt to use the
outer range of pitches—soprano or bass. While the songs were joyous, occasionally funny, they were never loud, so the hunters could can sing their
many songs for long periods of time. William Jack remarked: "I know a lot
of songs, I could sing all day." Joseph Rupert said, "You won't be able to leave
this place if I sing all my songs."

RHYTHMIC ELEMENTS

The songs were sung quickly, with the words winding intricately around a
light, energetically flexible beat, producing their own independent rhythm.
The rhythmic subtleties reflected the polysynthetic nature of the Cree language. Some beats were dense with notes and others had a single note and
syllable. I can cite no example of a *ritardando*, but it was not uncommon for
the music to accelerate, usually at the end of a pattern. Generally, the songs
in my collection of recordings are isorhythmic, consisting of a series of
equally stressed pulses. Within this predominant rhythm, there is often a
grouping of two pulses with the accent on the first of the pair, whether at

the same or different pitches. This rhythm gives the songs a forward-moving impetus. These rhythmic pairs seem equally to be a textual pairing of syllables that I indicate with a hyphen, e.g. *ah-pah*. However, such a pairing is not consistent with the intonational patterning of Cree. Linguist Roy Wright (1984) suggests there may be a relationship here to an old Algonkian linguistic pattern (i.e., phonological rule), because a similar alternating stress pattern is found in the spoken language of some Ojibwe dialects such as Odawa. Certainly, the Cree had communications with other peoples through trade and migration. Indeed, one elder said to me that much of Cree knowledge came from the east.

Moreover, the regular pulse set up by the singer is occasionally changed to give pronounced syncopation, or a change in how the word rhythm relates to the basic pulse. Joseph Rupert's "Trout Song," above, contains a good example of such rhythmic contrast.

Thirteen of the songs in my collection are metric-like, having patterns that fall regularly into double and triple divisions. Nine of the thirteen metric-like songs were sung by Mr. Pepabano, perhaps reflecting his love of the step dance done to fiddle music. The other four songs were sung by Samson Lameboy and, while metric, still retain much of the irregularity of pulse around breathing spots; they also have notes of uneven value. This metrical freedom is not characteristic of Euro-American music.

FORM

The form of Cree song is readily comprehended by Euro-Americans, for the songs are repetitive, and their sections are delineated by rests and melodic-rhythmic patterns. The largest repeated sections can be likened to verses, although the melody repetitions are never as exact as the non-Native expects in a written song.

Within the strophes are melodic-rhythmic units usually defined by breathing or rest points, although the "Partridge Song" (fig. 3.2) by George Pepabano shows patterns delineated not by rests but by an iambic rhythm created by rhythmic melodic movement as well as repetition of textual units. (Strophes are marked with roman numerals here; patterns within strophes with arabic numerals.)

> This song is about the partridge bird
> The partridge, and how he runs through the snow
> His feet are able to carry him through the snow on top, without sinking
> I compare myself to this bird, to a partridge
> When I have on my snowshoes I am able to run
> Like the partridge on top of the snow.

Figure 3.2: "Partridge Song" (Song 13), by George Pepabano

A number of the songs show a two-part AB form; the B section contains both rhythmic and melodic contrast. For example, Mr. Pepabano's "Partridge Song" is unified by the same compound rhythm, but in the B section the words (not shown because of their indistinct nature) are changed, the melodic contours inversed (A patterns descend, B patterns ascend), and a different gamut of pitches are employed (in the A section the pitches f, c, d are used; in the B section, e, b, c#, d#).

It is the smaller divisions, the patterns within strophes, that sustain most change among strophes. Yet the change is conducted in a controlled way so that the song remains unified at the verse level. Indeed, the change looks much greater than it sounds, for the ear hears the spinning out of blocks of similar sounds, rather than resting on each note and comparing, as the eye may do. The song changes varied in the same way over two years: the beginning pitch level, overall melodic shape, and tempi remained almost unchanged during the two years between the recordings of the repeated songs. Bruno Nettl (1965, 176) believes that there is a desire for variety in music which accounts for the large degree of variation of the short, simple phrases. On the other hand, unifying factors are of utmost importance in a society where all song relies upon oral memory.

Although Cree song is strictly monophonic, the pitches upon which the songs are based would not be dissonant if sounded together. This may be a result of acculturative forces, from the hymn-singing tradition, for example, but I believe it more likely to be an awareness of the natural consonance of certain pitches. Cree singers tend to sing the intervals most consonant in their frequency ratios such as unison/octaves, fifths, fourths, and major and minor thirds, in that order.

Several kinds of ornaments are an integral part of Cree melody. Appogiaturas (defined here as a quick note before the main note which does not alter the latter's position or time-value) often decorate the essential notes of a song. All but a few songs have vibrato on ornamenting notes. Vibrato is part of the melody in fifteen of the eighty-six songs I recorded. These may be a distinct type of song, because the sound ideal in these songs is a continuous flow of wavering pitches. As a consequence, the vibrato songs have music characteristics that set them apart from the other songs. First, although their melodies are typical of the hunting songs, they sound melodically level because the pitches merge into each other; second, they are sung with a softer vocal quality; and third, they have less rhythmic energy— often the pulse is obscured by long chains of pulsating repetitive tones as in William Jack's "Fox Song" (Song 2).

Prior to the song there is no experimentation with pitch, but rather a spoken sentence referring to the *nikamon* about to be sung. The sentence is enunciated loudly and quickly and leads directly into the song. The speech is in a conversational tone, not disruptive to the flow of the song, for the speaking and singing timbre of the singer's voice has the same qualities. Cree song supports musicologist Robert Erickson's statement, "In an oral tradition the sharp division between the categories of speech and music is often blurred" (1975, 98). Many of the spoken stories contain sung sections, and in the following story, two sections are chanted. I quote the entire story below. Notice also the emphasis on individual initiative, and the representation of animals as helpers.

Iashow's Story with Song
(told by Abraham Martinhunter, 1984)

You know that fish, it's really ugly; it looks like a catfish
That fish is a legend
This is the name of a man in the legend, Iashow

He tried to kill his son
He took his son to an island far away
Father said, "Go get the eggs for me"
The old man said, "Go gather the eggs, I forgot them"
The son didn't believe his father
He looked in the canoe; he went to get the eggs
His father left with the canoe
His father was already way out
The young boy started calling him, but he didn't come back
The young boy started throwing flat stones, skipping them across the
    water
He couldn't reach, the boat was too far away
All he had were the eggs
He broke them onto a stone to dry them out
That's how he would eat them—dried.
The seagull came and asked him why he was crying so much
Why he was filled with so much sadness
He hid under the wing of the seagull
He said, "My father has left me"
The seagull replied, "I can't help you"
During the night, the seagull told him to walk around the shore
While he was walking around the shore he saw the big fish I told you
    about
It was a very big fish
He said, "I can't help you, because your father can see all around us"
He said, "Go up on top of a rock and look for a cloud"
He saw some clouds hanging up in the sky but he didn't mention it to the
    fish
"I'm going to try and get you out—look for a large rock"
The boy went on his back
"If I slow down hit me on the head with that rock"
That's what he would do when the fish was carrying him on his back
They heard some thunder. It was trying to kill the boy
The fish knew what was going to happen when he heard the thunder
Then the fish sighted land
The fish said, "What's the thunder saying?"
As they neared the land, the thunder got louder and louder
The boy had on a necklace
He took the necklace and put it on the fish and said,
"Try and get me out of here."
The lightning was all over the place
Lightning struck them as they were right on land
The boy jumped to safety

The fish went under water and the lightning struck right where they
　　were
He made a lot of things on the way
When he went to meet his parents where they were
The father had two wives
A long time ago people had many wives
The boy saw a bird on top of their tent
There were many camps in that area
The boy told his mother, "Here I am."
When the mother turned around she had a lot of sores on her face
The people there were all very mean because of the doing of the father
He said to his mother and two little brothers, "Let's get away from this
　　area
I'm going to try to get rid of the people here."
So that night his mother and two little brothers left because he said,
"This whole area is going to burn including the water."
So the man could hear his son singing away that night
He made two arrows
This is the song he's singing about the water that's going to burn
And the fire that's going to help him

Figure 3.3: "Iashow's Song"

The boy asked his father to come out
The father said, "This is not the way you're singing"

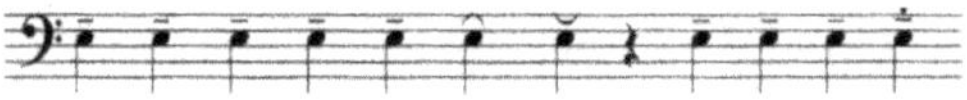

Figure 3.4: "Iashow's Song," continued

The old man said, "The water's not going to boil and the canoes burn"
"Come on out father"
He took one of his arrows and shot it into the air and fire started
He saw the people going for their canoes
This one landed in the water
All the canoes were burned
The only area that wasn't burned was the area where he was standing
Everybody came running to him
So the fire started
It was so intense they had to get away from there
This one landed in the water

All the canoes were burned
The only area that wasn't burned was where he was standing
Everybody came running to him
So the fire started
It was so intense they had to get away from there
See what they did to his father
Everybody burned but the boy
Children were very respected a long time ago
He brought it on himself for what he did to his son
"Cush, cush, cush, cush, cush, cush" (imitates robin sound)
So he changed his mother into a robin
He said, "I'm going to make you look nice, because you are covered with
    sores
From the old lady who was really mean to you"
And he changed his brothers into the two little birds with red on their
    heads
"You're always going to be a robin, and see Native people being born"
The boy turned into this "tatahshow"
I'm going to be that bird in all four corners of the earth
This kind of bird is a very beautiful bird.

At the end of the story, Abraham Martinhunter added this: "Children were respected a long time ago. Iashow brought it on himself, for what he did to his son" (Martinhunter 1984).

The Cree Sound Ideal

A typical Cree hunting song may be described as follows: the rhythm is organized as a quick one-beat metre and is dense with pitches of short duration. In some songs the mono-pulse rhythm is subtly grouped into patterns of two pitches. Although difficult to establish without the interplay of the drum, syncopation occurs in the songs; otherwise, the songs contain few accents. The range is narrow and seldom are more than five discrete pitches used. One pitch, through repetition, dominates the song, becoming a focus tone. Melodic embellishment is integral, particularly the appogiatura, which takes its durational value from the preceding note. There are a few instances of portamento, but generally the pitches are attacked cleanly. Vibrato occurs as an embellishment in most of the songs; although some songs have continuous vibrato. The form of the songs is characterized by repetition. The largest sections are strophic-like and of varying length. At the strophe level, the form remains stable. Within the shorter patterns, change occurs, such as the addition or deletion of patterns.

Figure 3.5: "Trout Song"—Song 4 (1982) and Song 58 (1984), by William Jack

Even the same songs repeated two years later are unchanging in pitch and overall content, only minor rhythmic changes were made as shown in the notated songs in figure 3.5.

The Cree voices I recorded were extremely individual in quality, which perhaps reflects the solitary life of hunters and trappers. Just as there are no chords, so there are no choruses. Moreover, there appears to have been sincere acceptance of diversity in sound, and it was accepted that every hunter had his own songs and way of singing. While I heard no discussion of music aesthetics, I did hear praise for those contemporaries who have a good memory for the stories and songs.

There is a Cree sound ideal, and how it would have developed if not suppressed, we will never know. Every hunter sang, and it seems to me each took great pleasure in creating these compact poems about animals set to song. However, the songs were part of a tool kit, and their practical functions appear to have outweighed aesthetic considerations. The songs lived on in the singer's mind for a lifetime, and were passed on to the succeeding generations to the end of the twentieth century.

4

Hymns and Hunting Songs

By the early twentieth century, the open fire has been replaced with a small stove and the migiwap is now a one-roomed wooden house, although most houses have a migiwap nearby for cooking the geese over an open fire. The family still gathers around the wood-burning stove and the grandfather sings a few of his hunting songs but, at the last syllable, he takes his treasured hymn book out of its colourful fabric bag and the family joins him to sing their favourite hymn in Cree, "The Great Physician."

 ✌

In the early 1980s, when I asked northern Cree elders to sing an old song, several responded with either a hunting song or a Christian hymn in the Cree language. Now, in this twenty-first century, the hymns, as well as the hunting songs, have been largely supplanted by the driving rhythms of the new gospel tunes. In this chapter, we explore why and how the hymns and gospel tunes have become musical descendants of the hunting songs.

Despite the beat of gospel music on the radio station, and despite the fact that few people must hunt for subsistence or trap for a livelihood, the hunt remains at the core of Cree ethos in subarctic communities. Listen to the people visiting in the northern malls in the spring and you will hear them discussing the quality of the geese flying overhead and who has their freezer full of them. With modern hunting technology, the hunting songs are no longer needed for a good hunt, and gospel music suffices.

While the animals remain the focus of local conversation, the songs and rituals for the hunt are all but gone. Speaking of the youth in Chisasibi, George Pepabano said, "Their way of living is different. It's not their living, those songs" (1982). Most attribute the loss of the drums and songs almost entirely to the work of Christian missionaries, but, as mentioned in chapter 2, the way was well prepared for the Christian message before the

H.213 N.		
1.	Pa-shoch i-tac nu-to-ko-lon	The great Physician now is near,
	Ka-sha-wa-ti-sit Chee-sus	The sympathizing Jesus,
	Ay-we mi-nu-wa-che-i-wat	He speaks the drooping heart to cheer,
	Ka-sa-ki-i-tuk Chee-sus.	Oh, hear the voice of Jesus.
	Chorus.	
Chorus:	Ma-wa-che mi-lo-ta-kwun	Seetest note in sereph song,
	Ot i-shi-ni-ka-so-win	Sweetest name on mortal tongue,
	Chee-sus a-i-twa-ni-wuk	Sweetest carol ever sung,
	Chee-sus mi-lo Chee-sus.	Jesus, Blessed Jesus.
2.	Wa-pa-li-tum mu-chi-twa-win	Your many sins are all forgivenm
	O-nu-to-tu-wik Chee-sus	Oh, hear the voice of Jesus;
	Ku-kwa o-ti-tu-mwak i-tat	Go on your way in peace to heaven,
	Ki-chi we-cha-wak Chee-sus.	And wear a crown with Jesus.

Figure 4.1: "The Great Physician" hymn and syllabary (and English translation) (Clarke 1974, 117)

missionaries arrived. Indeed, changes to Cree ways of life prior to missionary activity made an alteration of the Cree worldview inevitable. By the time the Anglican missionaries arrived in the nineteenth century, the songs and the dreams connected with them were no longer essential to the hunt.

This does not mean people had stopped believing in the old ways. To this day, most Cree affirm the power of the dreams and song, and speak of them with respect; in fact, one of my translators refused to translate portions of an elder's description of the shaking-tent ceremony. Some, who have experienced the power of the shamans, feel that they misused their powers, and express the hope that these sorts of activities remain in the past. A few think that the powers the elders held should be revived, often in tandem with Christianity, for the spiritual awakening of First Nations people.

Missionaries and Cree Song

The missionaries, especially the Methodist missionaries who came from a tradition of congregational song, recognized immediately that Cree spirituality was evoked through songs and through dreams. Vera Fast writes, "From earliest missionary endeavours the Indian love of singing had been harnessed to purposes of evangelism, and in the nineteenth century all missions utilized it to greater or lesser extent" (Fast 1983, 99). Bishop Provencher went so far as to insist that "a priest who could not sing would not be esteemed by the Indians" (220), and Reverend James Evans printed two thousand pages of hymns in Cree before he prepared the Lord's Prayer, the Creed, and the Commandments.

Literacy was important to Protestant Christians who believed that each individual should be able to read the Bible. To this end, as mentioned earlier, Reverend James Evans of Norway House devised the syllabics in 1840, a writing system that represented the sounds of the Algonquian language and provided the Cree with a compelling spiritual resource. An effective new way to transmit song had been introduced to northern peoples, and both the Cree and the missionaries of northern Manitoba took readily to reading and writing with the syllabics. By 1842, two Indians from Fort Severn on western Hudson Bay had introduced the syllabics to Moose Factory Christians on eastern Hudson Bay. Reverend George Barnley, who was serving as a Wesleyan Methodist missionary, then adopted the syllabics (Long 1986, 318), and Barnley's successor, John Horden, "saw at once that the syllabic system of writing had gained a decided foothold among the Cree of James Bay" (322). Historian Olive Dickason writes, "The use of the syllabary spread with amazing rapidity throughout the Cree-speaking North, so that by the end of the nineteenth century and the early part of the twentieth the Cree had one of the highest literacy rates in the world" (1992, 241).

The syllabic texts must surely have helped Reverend W. G. Walton ("Reindeer") curtail the drumming and the shaking-tent ceremony. He adhered strictly to Christian doctrine in his sermons in Fort George. On the other hand, during his thirty-two-year stay (1892–1924), he learned the Cree language and provided material aid to reinforce his efforts in the spiritual domain. Of Walton's work, Abraham Martinhunter said the following in 1984:

All the things Reverend Walton said would happen, have happened
When he first saw a plane, when the guns came
Everything Reverend Walton saw in the future, happened
A lot of white people would come and there would be vast change.

A century later, in the 1980s, the old people still relied on the syllabic writing of the hymns. With few exceptions, the elderly Cree of Chisasibi would request that the Walton prayer book and hymnary be brought to them before they would sing. One elder said, "I can't sing a hymn without looking at a book."

In addition to the authorized hymnaries, the Anglican missionaries chose hymns from evangelical and children's volumes such as Sankey's *Sacred Songs and Solos, Hymns Ancient and Modern, Golden Bells*, and *Alexander's New Revival Hymns.* The preface to the 1861 volume *Hymns Ancient and Modern* gives insight, reminiscent of Amtmann's observations cited earlier, into why these hymns proved so musically suitable for use by the subarctic Cree. First, the compilers explain the presence of unbarred melodies from ancient sources which, much like Cree songs, are "incapable of being expressed in ordinary symmetrical form" (p. iv). Second, the compilers state that the speed at which the hymns are sung should be left to the individual judgement of the choir director. This, too, would suit Cree hymn-singing, which is noticeably slow. Third, they state that the pitch of the hymns may depend upon circumstances; again, a comfortable approach for the Cree, who tend to sing hymns at a very low pitch. And finally, they point out the preponderance of long notes at the end of phrases, a practice that was readily adopted by the Cree (p. v).

But it was Ira D. Sankey's song collection, *Sacred Songs and Solos*, that was to have profound and long-lasting consequences for Cree musical spiritual life. A list of Cree hymn favourites in Chisasibi made by the Anglican priest Reverend Locke (see Appendix I) shows that the missionaries chose hymns with tunes that are easily learned and remembered. Approximately one-third of the favourite tunes listed in Appendix I were selected from the aforementioned *Sacred Songs and Solos*. Steve Turner writes, "*Sacred Songs and Solos* was the defining hymn collection of late nineteenth-century Evangelicalism" (2002, 135).

The singable tunes and straightforward message of Sankey's hymnary gave his work universal appeal. Yet, depending on the clergy involved, translations of hymns from English into Cree could undergo substantial changes such as greatly reduced vocabulary and simplified religious concepts. These outcomes and the processes producing them deserve further study. Nevertheless, Sankey's hymns were widely published and distributed, and have remained an inspiration for evangelical hymn singing.

The Cree use of the hymns paralleled non-Native use in many ways: for example, Abraham Martinhunter described singing "The Great Physician" from the Sankey hymnal to calm the turbulent waters of Hudson Bay. Two hundred years earlier, and on a different continent, John Wesley described his adoption of Moravian hymn-singing to deal with turbulent waters: "when, during a severe storm that terrified most of their passengers, the Moravian missionaries calmly stood on the deck singing their hymns entirely unperturbed by the raging storm and towering waves" (Chase 1966, 44). What was begun by John Wesley (and earlier by Martin Luther) and Ira Sankey has become the foundation of twenty-first century Cree Christianity—but not without some substantial music-rearranging by the Cree, as we shall see.

Indeed, many concepts in the hymns fit well with Cree life and spiritual beliefs. Historian Ken Coates says, "Native and non-Native spirituality were not as different as is commonly believed" (1991, 123). As they discussed the hymns, the elders liked to point out the similarities between Native and Christian beliefs.

Before religion came a long, long time ago
People still lived like Christians
They had a really good life they followed. (Bearskin, 1984)

And Samson Lameboy said: "The Cree believed in God before the minister came" (1984).

All of the hymns mentioned in this section are listed in Reverend Locke's list of frequently sung hymns in Chisasibi, Quebec, and it was still in use in 1984 (see Appendix 1). One of these, the aforementioned "Great Physician," was sung, as stated earlier, by Abraham Martinhunter to overcome the turbulent tidal waters of the bay. Many of the Cree who live on the coast have experience working on freighters in James Bay. These people understand the many references in the hymns to water, and mention of rough seas is frequent in the list of the favourite Anglican hymns in Chisasibi (the place name actually means "Big River"):

When peace like a river attendeth my way
When sorrows like sea billows roll (Sankey 1944, Hymn 901)

Jesus calls us; o'er the tumult
Of our life's wild restless sea (*Hymns Ancient and Modern* 1861, Hymn 225)

In the walking-out ceremony, the Cree blessed their one-year-olds before the children took their first steps on the ground outdoors. Job Bearskin cited this as an example of Christian-like religious behaviour that preceded the arrival of missionaries.

They followed the life of religion—
Look at the walking-out ceremony. (Job Bearskin. Interview by author.
Tape recording. Chisasibi, 1984)

In any case, such formalized cherishing of children would have prepared Cree people for the many hymns with a similar focus:

Little ones to him belong,
They are weak, but he is strong (*Cree-English Anglican Hymn Book* 1974, 135)

The many hymns that refer to a Supreme Being must have been compatible with the Cree idea of a Great Spirit, who was offered the first game killed by a youth, or some meat from the meal. Hymns also make frequent reference to early morning, a sacred time for the hunter (as described earlier in Joseph Rupert's "Trout Song").

Holy, Holy, Holy, Lord God Almighty
Early in the morning our song shall rise to Thee. (*Cree-English Anglican Hymn Book* 1974, 33)

Dark was traditionally a time of danger for the Cree, when the *bodwich* (bogeyman) could be heard. Well-loved hymns such as the following, from *Hymns Ancient and Modern,* must have offered comfort:

> Thou whose Almighty Word
> Chaos and darkness heard
> And took their flight. (Hymn 526)

Like the songs of the spirits in the shaking tent, the hymns affirm the future:

> Fear not! God is thy shield
> And He thy great reward
> His might has won the field
> Thy strength is in the Lord. (Sankey 1944, Hymn 811)

Laren Olsen (2001) suggests that it is likely that the invocations to the guardian spirits in the shaking tent became hymns calling upon Jesus and Mary:

> **Verse 4:**
> Never did I so adore,
> Jesus Christ, Thy Son, before
> Now the time! And this the place!
> Gracious Father, show Thy grace. (Sankey 1944, Hymn 491)

Dreams are another area of common ground:

> **Verse 3:**
> Was ever on your tongue such a blessed theme?
> Let us hear you tell it over once again;
> Tis ever sweeter far than the sweetest dream,
> Let us hear you tell it over once again. (Sankey 1944, Hymn 898)

The many songs about singing would resonate with any Cree hunter:

> All people that on earth do dwell.
> Sing to the Lord with cheerful voice (*Hymns Ancient and Modern*, Hymn 316)

> **Verse 3:**
> Oh, if there's only one song I can sing,
> When in His beauty I see the great King,
> This shall my song in eternity be,
> "Oh, what a wonder that Jesus loves me!"(Sankey 1944, Hymn 38)

Like many of the followers of Christianity, and indeed, of most religions, the Cree of Chisasibi believed that magical power resided in special locales. One such place was a mountain considered to be the centre of the earth. The mountain, created by the ancestors, was a source of good and of evil power, for this was the home of the *bodwich*. Another special locale, the site of malevolent monsters, forms part of James Bay near the community of Great Whale River. One elder described the waters there as dangerous and strong, going round and round. This was where Abraham Martinhunter sang the hymn "The Great Physician" for those who became ill.

The Cree elders I interviewed discussed other aspects of traditional belief and how they fit with Christianity. For example, the shaking tent constructed for the shaman's use was a sacred place, and from my conversations with the Cree, their dwelling tents also became, on certain occasions, places of sacralized time and space. The church as a sacred place was readily understood, and even assumed without needing explanantion.

Rocks were special in the subarctic Canadian shield area. Huge rock outcroppings were decorated with petroglyphs and pictographs, often depicting animals, animal-like creatures, and shamans with special powers. It was thought that little people lived in these rocks, occasionally to be sighted from boats. No wonder the hymn "Rock of Ages" speaks to northerners:

> Rock of ages, cleft for me
> Let me hide myself in Thee
> Let the water and the Blood
> From Thy riven side which flow'd
> Be of sin the double cure
> Cleanse me from its guilt and power (*Hymns Ancient and Modern*, Hymn 467)

The church graveyard, too, is believed to be sacred, and like Native special locales, it is viewed with mixed feelings. The Cree believe that the spirits of the dead, who have potential for harm, reside there. Brush is placed around new graves so the ghost of the recently deceased can be heard leaving them. Fear prevents people from going to a graveyard after dark, or picking the berries growing in the cemetery. Samson Lameboy (1984) described the traditional Cree belief in the spirits of the dead living on, but said that this was celebrated in the past, in contrast to the intense mourning of the present:

> A long time ago, my great grandfather heard that when people died,
> They didn't mourn
> They were singing and happy about the death

In the night they would wait for the spirit
They would put nets all around the camp so it wouldn't pass
They were waiting, they were waiting
I'll give you an example
They were happy.
A young man lost his father
Toward the evening they were happy, shooting their guns
Nowadays people mourn, everybody cries when somebody dies
They were very powerful at that time, the Bible was not around
The Bible says a lot of things now
They should mourn and things like that
They were very powerful, through hunting
Sometimes a man killed nothing because of the power somebody did on
    him
And sometimes he killed because of their powers

Despite this difference between the Cree and Christian traditions, there is a resonance in the idea of a spirit living on, an image in many hymns:

Verse 3:
Only "a little while" shadow and sadness
Then in eternity sunshine and gladness
Only "a little while" then over the river
Home, rest, and victor palm
Life, joy, forever. (Sankey 1944, Hymn 947)

The elders respected Jesus, for he was a man who had powers. The fasts of Christ are readily comprehended by the older Cree, who have memories of hunger, a major concern before the coming of government protection:

40 days and 40 nights,
There was fasting in the wild
(*English-Cree Anglican Hymn Book*, Hymn 94)

Jesus encouraged people to share, which is also an imperative of Cree society. Sharing through feasting was a common practice:

Hail sacred feast which Jesus makes.
(*Hymns Ancient and Modern*, Hymn 280)

The Cree have stories that emphasize the necessity of sharing; reciprocity was expected, and a person who did not give a fair share could fall victim to the sorcery of the ill-treated person. Following is a story experienced by an elder which illustrates the necessity of sharing:

When I was born, we dried our fish to save for the winter. When we were in the bush, all of a sudden I started crying for nothing. My grandfather said, "What's the matter with him? Why is he crying all of a sudden?" Then he said, "I bet you I know why he is crying, because somebody wants some of that." The mother said, "You know I saved some dry fish for him, I made a box for him." The old man said, "I want to give all that fish away." While my mother was doing that, she found some hair tied together in the box. This was the hair of the man who made him [Samson] sick. So they had to give it all away, they could make somebody angry. (Lameboy 1984)

Breath was important traditional Cree belief. Magic sticks propelled by a breath could fly through the air, destroy the enemy, and return to the thrower. Powder was blown in the direction of a person one wanted to die. Job Bearskin stated: "Natives blew everything; that's how the earth was created" (1984). Likewise, in Christian belief, the separable soul symbolized by breath is a central idea; Christians believe that all people partake of the breath of God, which leaves the body at death: "Saviour breathe an evening blessing" (*English-Cree Anglican Hymn Book*, 5).

The hymns mentioned here are the ones the Cree enjoyed singing, and in many cases still enjoy today. The common ground between these hymns and the traditional beliefs is an important point to remember. As the historian Ken Coates writes: "It is very clear that there was no rapid or unthinking acceptance of the new faith as has often been asserted" (1991, 123). Indeed, conversion was never as complete as church leaders hoped. While many hymns had concepts agreeable to the Cree, Reverend Andrew Wetmore observed that some were rejected outright, although he did not know the criteria used to judge them. Certainly some hymns have facts that may have been as puzzling (or perhaps fascinating) for the Cree hunters as for many Canadians. One song not listed as a favourite was "Awake! Awake! O Christian" (*Cree-English Anglican Hymn Book* 1974, 123), which uses the names of distant lands of the British Empire:

Verse 3:
From sea girt Australasia,
Where in the starry sky
The Southern Cross burns brightly

[And Verse 4:]
Neath India's glowing sun

All four verses of "The Gate Ajar for Me," meanwhile, are built around the idea of a gate open for those who accept the cross. There are, however, very few gates in Canada's North (Sankey 1944, Hymn 372).

Adapting Hymns to Suit Tradition

The Cree changed both the music and the hymn performance to conform to the Cree way of singing. The latter observation is reinforced by Reverend Wetmore (who worked with the James Bay Cree from 1978 to 1982) and through the recordings I made. During choir practice, Reverend Wetmore observed that the Cree strove very hard to capture the meaning of the words, but once this was accomplished, there was no further concern for blending the voices, for achieving a unison sound. Nor did they learn to sing in harmony, despite his attempts to teach part-singing during choir practices. Indeed, I attended one service where the women choristers were grouped on one side of the altar and the men on the other. The congregation had great difficulty joining in because the women's singing lagged noticeably behind the men's.

This lack of interest in group singing is not surprising, because until recently, the hunters and their families lived in relative isolation for much of the year, joining with others only in spring and fall. This isolation may also explain the unique vocal quality of each singer, and the lack of judgement about how one sounded to others. The Cree hunters believed that everyone could sing for hunting success. While several elders admitted that they sang better as youths, this may refer to breathing and volume, rather than to voice quality. In any case, there is no cultural imperative to have everyone sound alike, a Cree sound ideal that has passed into their hymn-singing.

Moreover, the contrast between the vocal timbres used for hymns and for hunting songs is strong. Hymns are sung in a loud, rhythmically static, nasal voice (women more so than men) characteristic of early Protestant hymn-singing, while hunting songs are sung in a quiet, rhythmically quick, soft voice.[1] A clue in the records of Francis Fletcher, the chaplain on Sir Francis Drake's ship in a 1579 voyage along the shores of northern California, explains the adoption of this different timbre for hymns: "whensoever they resorted to us, their first request was commonly this, 'Gnaah,' by which they entreated we would sing." Musicologist Gilbert Chase suggests that this may have been an imitation of the English singing through their noses, and that this tradition was transmitted to New England in the seventeenth century (Chase 1966, 6). Perhaps at the same time, hymns were being heard by northerners along the shores of Hudson and James Bay? If so, the peculiar vocal quality used for psalm-singing, and later hymn-singing, has been part of North American history for almost four centuries, long enough to become an enduring quality.[2]

There is more evidence to support the survival of Cree music practice as they interacted with missionaries. Reverend Wetmore noted that certain people had proprietary rights to particular hymns, manifested as the right to start the hymn. He speculated that this right was granted because the hymn "owner" knew the best pitch on which to begin singing. Reverend Wetmore acquired ownership of his own hymns because he introduced them to the congregation (1983). This practice is in keeping with tradition, in which the old songs are "owned" and sung only by their composer or by a chosen relative. Cree songs are personal, and generally are not sung by the community: the precise words are incomprehensible even to other hunters of the same generation.

As religious music, hymns and hunting songs also share some music qualities, such as the use of free rhythm and the use of syllabic text (one pitch per syllable) and, importantly, the similarity of function, for Cree song is spiritual song. Surely these affinities facilitated the missionaries' settings of the hymns and canticles of the liturgy into Native languages. There is speculation (192) that religious texts were adapted to Native melodies, but little supporting evidence exists for this in the Canadian north. One hymnal preface, written by Reverend Horden, contains hymns intended to be chanted, but the source of the chants is not given (Horden, undated). Would the clergy use Indian tunes in church?

The Cree applied elements of traditional song-making directly to the hymns. For example, Reverend Wetmore stated that the Cree singers ignore metrical patterning (regular patterns of accents such as those which distinguish a waltz from a march). Certainly, the rhythms of the hunting songs are patterned not according to metre but by word-tune units. In similar fashion, the eleven Cree hymns I recorded have no regular metre, just a continuous one-beat rhythm, rendered irregular by a subtle lengthening and shortening of note values and rests, and speeding up near the ends of word-tune phrases. One can speculate that sending a convincing message in song is more important to the Cree than the filling of time with a prescribed metre.

As we have seen, the hunting songs are strophic, like the hymns, meaning that the tune repeats with new words for each verse or repetition. Thus the structure of the hymns would be congenial to the Cree. The old songs, though, are less melodically conformist in their repetitions than are the hymns. As the words change, the tune and rhythm may be slightly altered to fit the words.

Lastly, hymns are fundamentally similar to hunting songs in that they have melodies that tend to be built on triads (three pitches sounded simultaneously), and which centre around one pitch, a sort of focus tone for the song. However, the elders slide between the pitches of the hymns, which contrasts with the hunting songs, in which they move quickly, lightly, and cleanly between pitches.

To sum up: the Cree integrated Christian hymns into their traditional lives by making changes to essential elements, such as the rhythm, but retaining the strophic form and tonal selection, and embedding the new music practice in the old ways. Because of their conformity to the Christian style of presentation, mainly the vocal quality of the hymns, their adherence to Christian ways was easily overestimated by outsiders. Those such as Reverend Wetmore, who worked more closely with the Cree and their music, were quite aware of the resilience of Cree culture, of its ability to absorb new ways that fit old practices.

Thus, Christianity and Christian hymns fitted well into the sacralized world of the Cree. By the twentieth century in northern Manitoba, elders were devout Christians and looked forward to the visits of the ministers who came only on special holy days, travelling in the summer by boat and in the winter by dog team. The regular Sunday services were presided over by respected elders. These catechists also served as intermediaries with the Cree population, and at the same time were often experienced practitioners of Cree traditions.

Elders tell of risking their lives to cross swift-flowing rivers in birch-bark canoes to attend summer services. Families often brought packed lunches, built a fire along the riverbank to boil water for tea, and visited with relatives and friends after the service. No one worked on Sunday, and children were not allowed to play. Everyone dressed up. Women and girls wore dresses and covered their heads for services.

The interplay of hymns and traditional songs provides an illustration of how the northern Cree borrowed from, and adapted, the institutional trappings of the Christian church. They accepted, with some modification, hymns in which the singing was done for the benefit of all, and for communication with the spirit world. For the highly visible group ceremonies of the society, Christian ritual and songs were used rather than traditional Cree ones—not surprising in view of the strong missionary condemnation of Cree drums, dancing, and ritual. At a personal level, however, the hunters relied upon the old songs to communicate with the animals.

Subsistence hunting remained the "habitat" for the hunting songs. First, they were a means of personal expression for the hunter, and second, even if no longer essential, they helped create good conditions for attracting the animals. The hunters did not associate hymn-singing with hunting; several hunters stated that only the dreams and old songs created good hunting. In hymns, the animals are domesticated, and wild animals, when cited, are described negatively. Indeed, there is none of the traditional ecological knowledge in the hymns, in contrast to the hunting songs that show reverence for the animals. The following lines from a hymn characterize wolves differently from the kind of wolf who might appear in a hunting song:

Men scorn Thy sacred Name
And wolves devour Thy fold. (*Hymns Ancient and Modern*, Hymn 370)

This incompatibility with the perspective of an individual hunter may explain why the hymns replaced only public aspects of Cree worship, while hunting songs survived unchanged into the 1990s.

Gospel Music

As mentioned earlier, gospel music originated with Ira Sankey, and has been described as "singing the Gospel." These lively songs became known as gospel songs to differentiate them from psalms and hymns. This music has become the foundation of Cree Christian life. Gospel music has appeal to those seeking addiction-free lives and striving to maintain strong family ties. Regular Cree services are now centered around it. Some evangelists even believe that the Gospel can be presented entirely in song, which expresses emotional truth better than speech. Often the Cree have no official preacher, just a series of singers, usually with a guitar, relating their messages through songs with titles such as "God's Godly Concern," "Holiness of Marriage," and "Before I Saw My Life."

Following is the Cree version of "Amazing Grace" contributed in 2004 by Robert Castell, Pukatawagan, Manitoba, from a collection of favourites written in Cree and as yet untitled and undated.

AMAZING GRACE

It is amazing: when I was lost, your love came to save me.

-1-
Mâmaskâcihtâkwan ôma
Kâ-pimâc'hikoyan;
Nîŷa ketimakisiyân,
Ni-kî-wanisinin.

-2-
O kisewâtotâkewin
Ni-kiskinoh'makon;

Ekâ'ẏa kita-kostamân,
Ni-wâpahtikosin.
-3-
Maci-paẏiwinihk âsay,
Ni-ka-pe-itahon;
Kesewâtisiwin ôma
Ka-wîcihikoyan.
-4-
Kâ-Tipeẏhiciket ani,
Ni-kî-asotamâk;
Miẏo-paẏiwin iẏikohk
Ke-pimâtisiyân.

Gospel songs share a similar form with the old songs and hymns. The vocal timbre remains intense and uniformly loud, as it is usually electronically amplified. In fact, the woman with the strongest voice usually starts the singing. Moreover, like the hymns, there is much sliding between pitches, which I suggest is a way of creating unending sound. But the old rhythmic flexibility is gone, and like country song, gospel music has strong metrical organization, usually propelled by the sound of rock-music drums. Like country songs, the words often tell a story with vivid and emotional images. Northerners attribute the words of the following favourite to a man from Split Lake, Manitoba, although the source is unconfirmed:

One night I had a dream
I was walking by the beach
There were two sets of footprints in the sand
One belonged to me
And the other to my Lord
He was walking beside me through this land

Though the number of participants varies considerably from community to community, gospel is a music which the people still *do* as opposed to *consume*. They take pains to translate and write it in Cree, and copy it on cassette tapes to be passed around so that songs may be learned by ear. It is sung at home, at healing gatherings, at wakes, at church, in the country or the city.

In keeping with past practice, the men usually play the accompanying instruments such as the electric keyboard and guitar. Like most traditional Cree gatherings, the time and even place of gospel events are not fixed, and attendance varies.[3] Gospel musicians may gather together simply to "jam" and speak to God with sung words rather than spoken.

Gospel became rooted in Cree life mainly through its use in wakes for the dead, which remain an integral part of Christian Cree ritual. Like most Cree events, these differ from community to community. In the past, wakes lasted from two to four nights, during which time the Cree would sing through the entire book of hymns, written in the syllabary. Now, wakes usually last for one day only. In one community, for example, taped gospel songs are played during the day, and in the early evening gospel singers arrive with their guitars and hymn books borrowed from the church. They begin by slowly singing tunes such as "Amazing Grace," "Till We Meet Again," "How Beautiful Heaven Must Be," and "Precious Memories." These are sung by the the regular Sunday church singers. At 9 or 10 p.m., the "Shakers" arrive with their faster and louder songs, which they sing until the early morning hours. After the wake, several favourite hymns such as "What a Friend We Have in Jesus" and "Sweet Bye and Bye" are sung at a church service presided over by a priest. Afterwards, all go to the grave, where hymns are again sung during the interring of the body. For these grieving songs, accompanying instruments are usually only a soft acoustic guitar and a bass guitar.

Like elderly people everywhere, older Cree resist changes to church music. In one predominantly Catholic community, they told me that they felt alienated when the Christmas songs were sung in English by a youth group. In Chisasibi, some elders remained faithful to the old hymns, and resisted the introduction of new hymns and gospel songs into the Anglican church, which indicates not only the power of habit but also a deep commitment to the hymns listed in Appendix I. It is not only the older people who feel this, however; I spoke with one younger person who said: "Maybe that's why we younger generation don't want to try, we don't want to change the wording, to mix them up. Because it's been passed down."

5

Country Music: How Can You Dance to Beethoven?

The children know that at dawn they will hear the old hunter's voice as he begins the day with a joyous song about the goose whose wings rattle like a song when he lands. Soon after, they hear their grandmother singing an ancient song as she carries water and wood into the dwelling for the new day.

As the day progresses, the children try tuning the radio that rests in a large cabinet made substantial by dry-cell batteries as bulky as today's car batteries, with an attached ground wire running to a high aerial. By late evening, they are able to pull AM stations from the southern United States, from Del Rio, Texas, from Waterloo, Iowa, from Omaha, Nebraska. The whole family enjoys the country music of Hank Williams, Jimmie Rodgers, and Kitty Wells. The English words are easy to understand, and the family relates to the everyday events described in the songs.

✦

When I asked a class of northern students in Thompson, Manitoba, why country music is so popular among Natives, a Cree student replied, "How can you dance to Beethoven?" Of course, country music is popular among non-Natives too, but its pervasiveness in Native society deserves investigation. For this discussion, the term country music is broadly defined to include commercial country music as well as country music with a western flavour (country and western), country music with a rock rhythm (country rock), and the fiddle music and jigging that are closely associated with country.

In 1981, I tuned in for one week to an evening music show broadcast on local radio CHTM, and kept track of the types of music offered. The show, designed for a Native audience, consisted of Cree and English announcements of upcoming events such as bingo, hockey tournaments, talent contests; there was also news on the condition of hospitalized persons, messages to persons on the trapline, and advertisements, the most memorable of which—for me—was the jingle for Kentucky Fried Chicken sung in Cree. I imagined hunters' jokes about this barnyard chicken with its own song! The music played on the show was largely country. During the week, I heard sixty country songs, three rock-and-roll, one traditional Native, and one popular.

The next year, 1982, I asked twenty Native students from across Manitoba to write down their favourite music. Eleven said they preferred country; four, rock and roll; two, classical; one, gospel; one, bluegrass; and one, folk. To compare, I asked a group of non-Native Manitoba students the same question, and the contrast was striking: country was not even mentioned. Seven preferred popular; two, classical; one, gospel; one, bluegrass; and one, jazz. Every year since 1982, a majority of my Native students have listed country as their favourite music; in 1999, sixteen of my twenty-one students preferred it.

But why do Natives express such a strong preference for this type of music? A decade ago, northern Manitoba elders barely understood the English language of the songs. When I asked one elderly hunter if he liked country music, he replied in Cree that if he understood the songs of the white man, he would probably like them, but since he didn't understand them, he got nothing from them. Even one of my young Cree students mistakenly interpreted a love song to be about sibling affection. Moreover, the roots of country music are in a rural, not a hunting way of life. An early type of country music was based on images of the northern plains, and performed by singing "cowboys." In Cree, there is no word for cowboy; they would say something like, "the man who rides on horseback." And no one actively encouraged the Cree to choose country music, as the missionaries encouraged the singing of hymns.

But we *can* find an explanation of the past and continuing popularity of country music in the history of interaction between Cree people and non-Natives. Even before learning the hymns taught by the missionaries, northerners heard non-Native music in the form of the songs and instrumental music from the explorers and traders. It's likely that some Cree heard the popular broadsides and folk songs of the day sung by the labourers of the fur-trade companies. Even much farther north, near Baffin Island, American whalers brought Hawaiian songs such as "Rolling Down to Old Maui" when they sailed between tropical ports such as Lahaina, Maui, and ports on the Arctic Islands (Brockway 2000).

Country music, like fiddle music, has its roots in the European songs brought to North America with the earliest immigrants. Indeed, many folk songs lived on in America after they were no longer sung in Europe. Even as Natives were hearing these songs and instrumental tunes, country was taking shape in the southern United States, a music that was to transform the northern Canadian soundscape. Before the 1920s, the music industry consisted of phonograph recordings and sheet music aimed at urban populations. Media owners were not interested in rural markets or rural music taste. However, improved radio broadcasting in the United States created phenomenal growth in the sales and popularity of the radio, and turned folk musicians into commercial performers.

Since the 1930s, powerful American radio transmitters have made commercial country music more readily available than any other genre of music in Canada's north. For many years, the clearest, and sometimes only, radio reception was of evening country music shows from the American South. Country singers became community favourites as families gathered around their radios. Later, local radio stations, such as CKDM (Dauphin, Manitoba) and the aforementioned CHTM (Thompson, Manitoba), developed shows combining country music with news and messages to those on the trapline from their family and friends at home. Northerners remember growing up with the sound of these stations; one student told of hearing country music every morning from five to seven as her mother did the chores.

The dedications on these radio shows deserve attention. I did not find one love song sung by a hunter to a woman. People did, however, call the station to dedicate commercial songs to loved ones. My students affirmed the Cree tendency to be non-verbal in romantic situations, and said that radio dedications give Native people a means of expressing these emotions. Sometimes the songs are just to let people know the sender is home or having a party. A Native broadcaster from CHTM said that most songs chosen for dedications are country, and that sometimes songs are even chosen to tease another person. For example, a girl may request a song like "You Ain't Woman Enough to Take My Man" and aim it at a rival. In another example of communication through radio dedications, one listener asked for Merle Haggard's "Take Me Back and Try One More Time," after which another listener called to ask the the broadcaster to play a song called "I Will." Occasionally, the dedications have become embarrassing in communities where everyone knows everybody else, and so, before the requests are played, they are reviewed by the radio committee in charge of programming.

When I asked students why they preferred to listen to country, they said that country music helps them relax and makes them feel comfortable, and has words that are both understandable and meaningful. Some mentioned the rhythm as being relaxing and soothing. Others said they listen to country because it is slow, because it has an even tempo and flows smoothly. They described the sound as soft, quiet, and mellow, with no high notes. Several people mentioned that country music is often sung solo, and that it is simple music. They said that, because of the clear words, they can relate to the singer's feelings. The country songs tell stories about everyday people, stories to which they can relate. They said that country is for dancing, singing, telling stories, and helping people to laugh or cry.

Country became the everyday music of the northern people for other reasons, too. The musical instrument most often associated with country music, the guitar, is relatively easy to store, maintain, and carry about in the remote settlements. It is also inexpensive and available to rural persons through catalogue sales. This applies to most other folk instruments as well, such as the harmonica. Some persons even made their own stringed instruments from materials at hand. Country music lends itself to aural, solitary learning, important qualities in areas without music instruction available. This approach fits the favoured Cree mode of cultural transmission: they learn by careful observation and by listening. Not infrequently, Native guitar players learned to play while hospitalized for tuberculosis for months and even years at a time.[1] One woman described how her aunt learned to play the guitar by ear. Her aunt would sing part of the tune and play the chords that she thought were appropriate for the song. If the notes chosen sounded right, she would keep them in mind and go on to find other chords for more of the tune. She learned how to play most of the chords by watching other people play guitar.

In addition, country music has important musical similarities to the hymns that Catholic and Protestant missionaries were intent on teaching. Surely the two genres reinforced each other as the Cree learned to understand and to participate in non-Native music. Hymns and country music are structured as verses with choruses. They have melodies that are repetitive and require only a few chords. Country tunes are usually sung solo, the preferred mode of Native singers.

Moreover, the high, wailing voice used in country music is similar to the vocal timbre used for hymns, in contrast to the gentle sound of the Cree hunting songs. It seems likely that the similar vocal intensity in early American folksongs, and later country music, may have had its roots in religious singing.

In both country and hymn music, Cree musicians freely vary the number of beats or pulses in each measure. Non-Native fiddlers and singers have great difficulty joining in, because the music does not begin after, or progress in, predictable four-bar phrases. Considering the strong metres in the commercial country music that the Cree hear, their apparent willing-

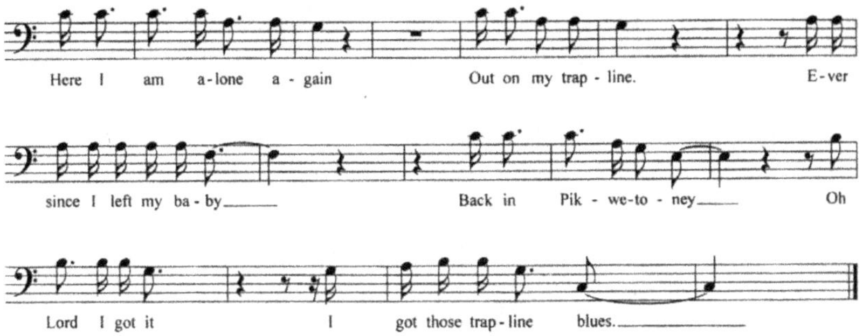

Figure 5.1: "Trapline Blues," a country song, Jack Brightnose, Cross Lake, Manitoba, 1980

ness to manipulate metre in their own renditions is striking, and perhaps reflective of their rootedness in oral tradition, wherein the effect of the sound is more important than regular organization of beats.

In addition to the flexible structuring of musical metre, the common setting for country music, urban bars, is unstructured and informal, definitely accommodating the cliché of "Indian time." For persons newly arrived in urban areas—and half of Manitoba's Aboriginal population now lives in urban centres—bars often replace home parties for socializing. To the non-Native observer, the constant movement of individuals in and out of northern bars is striking. There is no commitment to be at the bar at a certain time, or to remain there for a predetermined length of time. Everyone is welcome, but not criticized if they fail to show, or if they leave early. Clothing and seating is as informal as the use of time. These must surely be some of the qualities considered when the Cree students said they liked the informality of country music.

The informal social activity in bars is similar to the entertainment formerly enjoyed by people in the communities before radio reception, and before highways that facilitated alcohol consumption. Frequently, an impromptu dance would be called at someone's home. As word of the evening entertainment spread around the community, the hosts would busy themselves stacking their furniture in a corner, or even carrying it outside to make room. Most of the men in each family could play fiddle and guitar, and these instruments were always at hand, often hanging on the wall. The men would all take a turn playing to keep the music going throughout the night. The dancers also had to take turns because of the lack of space in the small dwellings. Some of these dances turned into non-stop weekend events. One group of dancers would dance for a few hours, then another group would arrive, allowing the first group to go home and sleep for a while. The nearest neighbour would supply the food and tea to everyone. People from other reservations nearby might arrive to join in. The music could be heard across the whole reserve on cold winter nights (Venne 1998).

Country music speaks to First Nations people, as it does to all who feel uncomfortable in urban society. The themes of family life, love, loneliness, and death have direct and immediate appeal. One student said that country music represents solid reality. It incites feeling, not cerebral appreciation of clever music structures and words. Many of those Natives who go to live in cities like Montreal or Winnipeg find it an uncomfortable experience. The following chorus and verse from the "Streets of Winnipeg," by northerner Jack Brightnose, is sung to the tune of "Streets of Laredo," and describes the unpleasant consequences of a Native person moving to an urban area:

Hey, ho
Way ya ho hey ho
Way ya ho ho-a-ho ha ho
As I walked down the streets of Winnipeg one day
As I walked down the streets of Winnipeg one day
I spied a young Indian wrapped in white linen
All wrapped in white linen and cold as the clay

Speaks with guitar accompaniment:
He staggered down the sidewalk in his unkempt clothes
With his shoulders stooped and his head bowed low
And his eyes that stare in defeat
With his three-day-old whiskers
And his body that smelled full of wine odour
Thinking to himself
Who am I? What am I?
You come to the big city
Because somebody said that life would be easier
Regardless of race, colour or creed
Regardless of race, colour or creed, huh
That's a laugh
Because in the big city
He can be accepted of his own kind
And all he could do is drink, drink and drink
And searching within himself the things of life
There are things that he could not understand
Why back home, why nobody dies of old age anymore
I remember when I was a child
And I believe in those things that I was taught. (Brightnose 1980)

Country music provides a bridge for the Cree between past and present ways of understanding the world. During the decades the Cree have listened to country, they have become multilingual and—in some cases—unilingual again, this time in English instead of the Algonquian language. There are many reasons for the adoption of English, such as its enforced use in residential schools. Country music has also exposed northerners to the English language in an accessible form, and surely must have reinforced English usage. Nevertheless, spoken English is still imperfectly understood by many Cree, but clearly country songs communicate well. They, like their folksong antecedents, have vivid images and repeated motifs that are clearly expressed.

The words of country songs describe acceptance of and resignation to the larger forces that control the lives of the average person, a quality in common with Christian music that emphasizes life beyond the grave. These words resonate with Cree people because of the fact that many aspects of their lives are now controlled by forces external to the Cree individual and their society. After contact, the Cree gradually lost control of local ways of being healthy and healing, of learning, and of surviving. Even as trappers, they were dependent upon non-Native fur markets controlled thousands of miles away on another continent. For some northerners, country music makes dependence palatable. It does not protest. It comes largely from the outside, to be consumed rather than created. Indeed, it has been described as music to drink by.

Occasionally amateur musicians use country music to poke fun at society around them. The "Auctioneer Song," for example, has been changed to re-enact the Native sale of land for beads. "Kaw-Liga," a love song about a cigar-store Indian who goes out with a wooden Indian maiden, has a line changed to "He would have gone with her, but didn't have the bus fare." Open protest is rare; examples include Brightnose's "Streets of Winnipeg," quoted above, and "I Want to Be Free," by Angus Monroe of Island Lake, Manitoba. These songs express the misery of Natives in urban society and their longing for the past, when the Cree lived in hunting communities.

Cree Contributions to Country Music

Since the 1970s, Cree musicians have played an active role not only in consuming but in making and selling country music. Some have become professional performers, making a further break from a tradition that did not consider music as something to be performed for an audience. A southern Manitoba band, C-Weed, has North American hit songs with "Evangeline" and "Run as One." Ray St. Germain, a Métis from Winnipeg, has had a number of international bestselling recordings. In the north, Leonard Constant from The Pas and Ernest Monias of Cross Lake have been models for youths to emulate. Ernest Monias' talent became known when he was chosen to accompany Ray St. Germain on a northern tour. There was huge demand for Ernest's first recording, a 45-rpm record called "Stay Awhile." Everyone in northern Manitoba has heard of Ernest.

Until the last decade, these northern singers and composers held on to essential elements of Cree music. They often used unconventional metres, and sang in Algonquian about topics of relevance to northerners. But, as these musicians, who were also avid music listeners, continued to absorb non-Native measured patterning of music, rhythms not derived from northern surroundings but from urban society, many of their performances have become rhythmically indistinguishable from those of non-Native country musicians. But the Cree remain firmly rooted in oral tradition. They write down song lyrics assiduously, but rarely do they write the music notation for the tunes.

There continues to be active lobbying for recording studios in the north. The musicians, with their idiosyncratic approach to rhythm, find it difficult to play with southern studio bands, and the expense of going south to record can be prohibitive. For example, Eric Sinclair of Cross Lake saved enough in 1981 driving a taxi (about $2,000) to go south for a few practice sessions and to make one recording. His own composition in waltz time, "As Long as Forever," was well received in the north.

As early as 1980, Eric Robinson, a Cree broadcaster for the Canadian Broadcasting Corporation (CBC), produced a one-hour upbeat show called "Country Music in Manitoba." Produced in Thompson, it featured a plethora of Native musicians, although, at the time, few were generally recognized as such: Bill Flammond, Robby Brass of the band Red Wine, Darren Ray Beck, and Len Henry of Boggy Creek. At this time, too, Native Communications Incorporated (NCI) radio was beginning to grow. It was initiated in 1971 by three northern Manitoba communities—Cross Lake, Wabowden, and South Indian Lake—and calls itself "the Voice of Aboriginal People." Now, with its country music programming and local news, it has become a staple in most northern homes and offices, and in many southern ones, too. Much of its funding comes from live talent shows, gospel jam broadcasting, and bingos. NCI has begun to produce television shows for the Aboriginal Peoples Television Network (APTN). In addition, most of the northern reserves are equipped with their own satellite receivers. The Nashville Network is *the* channel to watch.

In this new millennium, several of Ernest Monias' sons, such as Delaney and Orville, carry on the family music tradition, performing in a contemporary idiom that is rooted in country but combined with rock and blues sounds. Ernest's rhythm guitarist for ten years, Douglas Ross of Cross Lake, now records his own songs. They are like Ernest's, with solo voice, sometimes in Cree, accompanied by a few chords on guitar, and with Aboriginal themes involving the eagle, the drum, and *Manitou*. However, in some, an overlay of synthesized sounds creates a non-traditional effect: the rhythms are regular, there are harmony vocals, and his vocal quality is softer than country singers.

Douglas aims to achieve a synthesis of Native spirituality and Christianity in his songs. He uses instruments that will give him the sounds of Native tradition: the drum, the rattle, and the bass guitar, played to be the voice of thunder (2004). In one song, "Kitchi-Okimaw Kitimakinewin," Doug's voice takes on the wailing sound of the hymns. He chants in Cree: "Lord, have mercy upon us, always and forever." He sings this one during the sweat lodge ceremony. His songs combining Native and Christian elements bring to mind ethnomusicologist John Blacking's statement: "In certain social contexts important ideas can be expressed and fundamental changes of direction enacted through the practice of the nonverbal performing arts" (1995, 25), echoed further in 1981 in the words of one of my Native students about country music: "Doesn't it reflect where people are at? Isn't it like a moving picture of people?"

Country music has carried the Cree into the new millennium. In only a few generations, the northern Cree have moved from the songs of a hunting society to the mundane songs of contemporary society. Country music serves to create and maintain community around shared ideas of how individuals and families relate; it affords performers and listeners the opportunity to express themselves musically, as the Cree have always loved to do; and it connects isolated groups to the broader community. During much of this time of enormous challenges, country music has been there to help them express their feelings.

On the other hand, this music coming over the radio carried the rhythms and philosophies of the non-Native ways of the American South, whereas the hunting songs had incorporated the rhythms and sounds of the immediate experience of the northern physical environment.

Why has country music been so successful at replacing the old traditional Cree songs, more successful even than the Christian hymns and gospel music? The answer may have something to do with economics. In the 1980s, prices fell sharply for furs. Although prices had always fluctuated, this time they did not rebound, and the incentive to trap wild animals for a living was finished, perhaps forever, further distancing the Cree from the hunt. For many, the flexible rhythms of the hunting songs became the regular metres of country music; the soft chanting was replaced with the nasal timbre of country singing; individualistic vocal quality was replaced with a uniform "media driven" sound; the creativity of wordplay in the Cree language was lost in efforts to get the English words of the country songs right; and love songs directed to the animals and all living beings became love songs for, and about, the opposite sex. This was not just a matter of listening to and mimicking sounds; it was an internalisation of a new way of thinking about and living in the world.

Perhaps a story from Harry Hughboy of Wemindji, Quebec is the best conclusion.

> So he told the people to hang a pail up on the tree and so they did
> He asked the people to bring it down again
> In the pail, there was an organ from the child
> Then he asked the people to make him a shaking tent
> So they built him a shaking tent
> And he told everybody to turn every container upside down
> To turn all the canoes upside down
> Then he went into the shaking tent
> And made a lot of racket and noise
> There was an old woman in the camp
> When he sensed the place moving he went over to check the plate
> The Cheeoosoowash felt somebody
> Had checked one of the containers
> Already they were one-half full
> Of the ways of the white man's culture
> Then Cheeoosoowash said, "Tear the tent down it won't work anymore
> Because somebody has checked one of the containers
> From this time forth you people will experience hard times"
> Now that is how it is today
> We have the white culture coming in
> And we are experiencing hard times. (1982)

6

Powwow in the Subarctic

The little boy sat proudly beside his dad in the captain's chair of the big blue van. They sped by miles and miles of dense jackpine growth and rock outcroppings, but the long distances between communities went unnoticed by the two northerners. They were engrossed in the music from the cassette player propped up on the dash. The steady boom of the drum and the pulse of the van's engine worked together to intensify the feeling of forward movement.

The cassettes were well-used copies of northern plains drum groups such as the Tootoosis family or the Stoney Singers, and the songs were identified by the dance they accompanied: grass dance, war dance, round dance. Upon hearing a familiar tune, the father would sing confidently and full voiced; other times, less sure of the melody, he joined in whistle humming. He played the cassette over and over until the songs were learned.

Four hours later, when father and son arrived at The Pas, Manitoba, they could sing several new grass dance songs together.

Thus far, we have seen how the Cree made both hymn and country music their own, and how hymns can, in both musical and spiritual ways, be argued to be a descendant of the hunting songs. Now we look at powwow, a musico-religious movement that proclaims Indian identity and that is spreading through the subarctic. The Cree are adopting powwow song, but I have heard little evidence that they are putting their own musical stamp on it as they did with hymns, gospel, and country. They have, however, circumscribed the context of powwow music; it is mainly sung at small noncompetitive events such as the opening of a hospital or school.

Farther south, on the northern plains, a typical powwow gathering may last several days. They are held on different reserves on weekends throughout the summer so that they don't interfere with the regular work-days of attendees, who watch or compete in the Indian dancing. The danc-ing is accompanied by drum groups, each consisting of at least four singers. For publicity purposes, the size of the powwow is judged by the number of drum groups signed up, which, in turn, is often related to the size of the cash prizes available for the dancers and drummers. At one end of the cir-cular dancing and audience space there is a high stage from which the well-amplified comments of the master of ceremonies direct the proceed-ings. Judges, often previous winners, give points and select winners of the dance contests based on footwork, dance style, and dress.

The large powwows are run by the clock, and promptness is rewarded with extra points for those who participate in the Grand Entry. The visu-als, especially the colourful outfits, are compelling, but even more notice-able are the sounds, which emphasize the ritual aspects of the event. Most male dancers wear metal bells that create a noticeable effect when they move. For female dancers, there is a special dance called the jingle dance, performed in dresses with bells sewn on. When the drum begins, everyone stands for the solemn procession of dancers, who are arranged according to dress, sex, and age.[1] The Grand Entry is awaited in great suspense as the jingle of the bells on the outfits becomes more sustained and the bright flashes of colour begin to take on the completed forms of the dance outfits. The bearers of the sacred eagle staff (the Indian flag) and of the Canadian and/or American flags are usually war veterans. The flags, deposited in the centre of the dancing ground, are followed by a long circular chain of dancers who continue to dance until all are assembled. When the resplen-dent group becomes still, an elder offers a prayer. The master of ceremonies (MC) is responsible for keeping all this proceeding smoothly. He acts as a teacher, telling people what to do and explaining why they must observe certain rules of behaviour.

The dancing space is ringed by the audience and then by concessions selling both Indian food, such as bannock and Indian stew, as well as typ-ical North American fare, such as hamburgers and hotdogs, and all kinds of jewellery, clothing, and other items, mostly of Native origin. Sometimes there is a temporary shelter, set apart from the main dance group, where men play a traditional hand-game accompanied by the sound of hand drums. There may also be rides for the children.

What makes powwow, originally a Plains event, attractive to some dwellers of the subarctic? One explanation may involve the attack on Abo-riginal identity experienced by all Native peoples, including the removal of children to residential schools (breaking the cultural continuity between generations), and the construction of highways through communities to service hydro projects or mine sites—with the secondary result of alcoholism epidemics. In addition, communications media carried new sounds and new ideas into the subarctic, as we have seen—particularly country music but also the possibility of *choosing* an identity. For some, the choice was an "Indian" culture as exemplified by the powwow. One Cree leader (who preferred that his name not be used) offered me an explanation for Cree readiness to seek an identity from the outside. He pointed out that northern Cree identity is inherently weak because every northern village has its own background and culture, the villages are more or less grouped by families, and some communities have only four or five surnames within them. There is no *tribal* unity such as is to be found in the Alberta Indians. In addition, he added that northern Cree have been continually displaced by pressures from dislocated groups such as the Saulteaux (Ojibwe) to the east and the Chipewyan (Dene) to the north (Personal communication 1981). Indeed, as late as the 1980s, northern students would say to me, "We know we're Indians, but what tribe are we?" After finding out their home community, I could most often reply, "Cree."

Into this lacuna came "pan-Indianism," a term used by observers, rarely by participants. Pan-Indianism, for this discussion, fits the definition provided by anthropologist Robert K. Thomas:

> One can legitimately define pan-Indianism as the expression of a new identity and the institutions and symbols which are both an expression of that new identity and a fostering of it. It is the attempt to create a new ethnic group, the American Indian. It is also a vital social movement which is forever changing and growing. (1972, 128–29)

To those northerners seeking an identity, the powwow is a compelling introduction to an often-new "Indian" world.[2] Symbols of Indianness are everywhere, and ideas about Indian identity are forged and strengthened, as are personal relationships among members of diverse tribes. Thus, as an appealing social and ritual event, powwow has considerable persuasive power in winning Natives to the awareness and acceptance of a shared identity on a larger scale, it serves politically to unite the very diverse First Nations groups across Canada.

My thoughts on the powwow as a context for music began one hot day in July 1980, in Manitoba, when I drove to a powwow on the Sioux Valley reserve with a northern Cree friend named Margaret. She took a careful look around and remarked, "Nothing is Indian here, not even the Indians." We both laughed, for truly this flamboyant, competitive, and highly structured show was unlike any Cree event Margaret had experienced in the North. For the Cree, the Indian culture of the powwow is, in many ways, inimical to their heritage as subarctic hunters. The qualities necessary to conduct a successful powwow are inappropriate in a hunting society, where dependence upon wild animals renders useless rigid planning and routine work. Like the work situation of industrial society, the powwow is based upon a structured, competitive, bigger-is-better, technology-dependent model.

Southern powwows are planned over a long period of time by the coordinated efforts of many organizers. Commonly, band members meet two or three months before the powwow and elect a powwow committee headed by a president, vice-president, and secretary-treasurer. Other volunteers are assigned certain tasks, such as setting up the grounds. Fundraising continues throughout the year, and may come from a variety of sources—donations, money-raising schemes, leasing of land, and so forth. A committee member on the last day of a powwow in southern Manitoba indicated the value placed on planning and organization:

> Well, we're planning to start our committee early this year and do our promotional work before too long and we'd like to welcome everybody out here. And we hope that we have a better organization next year and we hope to have more people. We hope next year will be bigger and better. (Personal communication 1982)

The powwows begin and end at the specified hours. Competitors must be ready to begin their dance at the announcement of each event, and they file in and out on schedule. Most powwows have a standardized progression of categories, which are rigidly followed—each event immediately following the one before. Unlike the small Cree groupings, where events begin when everyone is ready, the powwow is run on the impersonal rigid demands of clock time. Furthermore, the large posters advertising the powwow usually state that registration for the competition closes, for example, on Saturday at 1 p.m., and with large cash prizes at stake, these requirements are strictly observed.

Contrast this use of time with that of an old-time northern Cree dance in Grand Rapids, Manitoba, which could be flexibly timed, at every point, to meet the needs of the people participating and to suit community occasions:

> Most of the dances were a spur-of-the-moment idea. It was only on rare occasions that a dance could be planned in advance. The people who would host the dance would tell one person and news would just carry through the town. (Personal communication 1981)

Also, the use of space at a powwow is delineated: there are spectators and there are performers. Although spectators are invited to dance, there is usually little response from those not in dance outfits. The powwow audience tends not to participate with foot-tapping. Even joking and talk is dominated by the announcer, who sits before a microphone and is elevated above the crowd on a specially constructed stand.

The drummers and singers may sit among the audience, but they form tightly knit groups around the drums, with their backs to everyone else. Although not unfriendly, they tend to withdraw from the crowd and to socialize only with other drummers or close family and friends. As mentioned earlier, the traditional Indian hand games are placed well away from the dance site, often behind the concessions. Even though they are accompanied by a small hand drum, I notice little intrusion of musical sound from the main dance area. The spatial compartmentalization of the powwow according to function, and the apparent attitude that the dancing, music, and even talk should be the domain of specialists contrasts with traditional subarctic music events such as a marriage dance, which include continual participation by everyone present, even the children. Marriage festivities include dancing, talking, laughter, foot-tapping, and continual movement through and around the dancing space. The boundaries between the dancers and audience space are flexible, as are their activities.

The competitive aspect of the larger powwows, where judges choose the winners, surely has its roots in the agricultural fair, where prizes are offered for best entries. Some mothers actively and aggressively encourage their children to dance and to vie for the judges' attention. Adult competitors dance long hours under the hot prairie sun because the more they dance, the more likely they are to catch the judges' eyes. This behaviour is consistent with the values of the dancers in a traditional Plains ceremony such as the Sun Dance, which also emphasizes discipline and endurance, but the rewards in the latter instance are spiritual, not financial.

Finally, none of this large-scale competition would be possible if not for modern technology. News of powwows is spread over the Internet. Powerful amplification systems allow the single bass drum and accompanying singers to be heard by hundreds of people—even thousands at the world's largest powwow, the Gathering of Nations, at Albuquerque, New Mexico. The MC announces the progression of events and the recipients of the giveaways (i.e., gifts, such as quilts, given to participants by families in order to honour the person or recognize a special event). Most significant, however, is his commentary. He constantly guides and advises the performers and spectators, and explains Native views and beliefs as they relate to the powwow activities. In effect, skilful announcers participate in the process of codifying a system of belief that defines the modern Native. Because these beliefs and the accompanying rituals are primarily an oral tradition,[3] different MCs offer different explanations. But there are also many similarities, and we may witness the emergence of an organized, formal doctrine as the powwow movement not only spreads but coalesces.

For example, if an eagle feather is dropped, not only does the MC demand that everyone stand for the Honour Song, but he may also explain the sacred nature of the feather and the respect that it must command, perhaps explaining that when an eagle feather falls from a dancer's outfit, it represents a fallen comrade in previous wars. To retrieve the feather, the "Eagle Feather Song" is sung. Four veterans, who represent north, south, east, and west, dance slowly toward the feather. As the song proceeds, there are four check beats (accented drumbeats); at each check beat, the veterans count coup—i.e., humiliate a foe by getting close enough to touch him— on the fallen feather. This represents the pushing back of the enemy so as to rescue their fallen comrade. Following this, the oldest veteran picks up the feather with an eagle stick, never touching it, and hands it back to the owner. The owner must pay the veterans for retrieving the feather, as well as the person who spotted the feather and the drum group that was chosen to sing "The Honour Song." In doing this, the owner is not paying for the feather, but honouring those who helped him retrieve it. After this rite, the drums return to the dance music and the competition resumes. Other interruptions occur throughout the day and evening, for special honour songs, giveaway songs, and non-competitive intertribal dances.

The role of women at the powwow appears to be following trends in North American society. Traditionally, women seldom danced, and if they did, it would be around the men, on the outside of the dancing space. They did not sing publicly, except for those wives, usually of war veterans, who were invited to join in at the descending phrases of the powwow tunes. Women are objecting to this subservient role, and there are now all-female drum groups even in the subarctic region. A well-known Dakota MC explained the traditional women's role this way:

> There are women that pick up the final verse and end it. When the men bring it to an ending it goes down, so the women pick it up from there. They are very important because they are the foundation of a home. So when a group gets together, their mothers and grandmothers are very important. And the women come in and sing along with the drum. It means a great honour for them, and we hardly see that any more. (Hotain 1993)

As yet, the dresses of female dancers fall below their knees. Although colourful, their clothing is indeed modest compared to male attire, as is their dance style. For example, during the woman's traditional dance, they remain stationary or move slowly, arms at sides, bending only their knees. Nearly all women carry a blanket draped over one arm, and the blanket must not be dropped. In contrast, the male outfit is extremely flamboyant, exaggerating the male physique. Male dance steps, too, are wide-ranging, aggressive, and expressive of individual personality.

There were, and continue to be, diverse reactions to these practices in the remote northern communities. In addition, many elders, influenced by Christian missionaries, have mixed feelings about sharing their beliefs. When asked about Cree traditions, some refuse to share their knowledge, and make jokes about wearing turkey feathers and the Great Spirit coming down. They say that the traditional hunting beliefs were hidden, and continue, if at all, in secret. One elder told me that the young fellows who are into "traditional" culture don't understand what they are doing. The few powwows he has been to bother him. He said that people who really know tradition keep quiet about it; there may be someone in the next room who knows more. He concluded by repeating that people now don't know what they are doing, don't understand the old ways, and ought to respect traditions by leaving them alone. Referring to the old ways, he said:

> It's fresh in my mind. I can sit here and think about it. I can still hear it. But I would never repeat it. No, because I'd be too embarrassed. They're bringing the powwows in, it's not part of this tradition at all. It's embarrassing the people and therefore they're drawing back. (Personal communication 1979)

And another comment:

> They used to get out the drum and hang it from the ceiling of the tent, and a couple of them would dance around. But they didn't do it as an exhibition. (Personal communication 1984)

Some youths who have become active in powwow reject Christianity. One youth said to me, "I never could get used to the sinner idea." This approach saddens many elders because Christianity has been the religion of many generations of Cree. Some, though, are able to combine Christian with pan-Indian beliefs, and note that the two have much in common, such as the idea of one Creator and the importance of addiction-free living.

There were, and are, mixed opinions of the powwow in northern Manitoba. The societal conservatives resist attempts to introduce Plains culture and to assume a shared Indian identity. They joke about the youths in

Indian dress, and cling to the ethos expressed in the Christian hymns and country music—an ethos shaped over decades to fit northern life. Other northerners, meanwhile, seek a new and strong "Indian" identity, and eagerly espouse the tenets of pan-Indianism, the trappings of Plains culture, and the dance and song of the powwow.

While much of the structure and content of the powwow is new to subarctic peoples, the oral method of imparting knowledge of the powwow is consistent with their Cree tradition. New oral narratives exist to validate the powwow's place in Cree culture. I spoke with three young powwow musicians who explained why they drum and sing, and their descriptions can be said to form part of such a new narrative.

All three sought their answers by returning to traditional Native values, such as respect for nature, contrasting them with the white man's values, such as alienation from and destruction of nature. At the heart of the powwow is the drum, which symbolizes Mother Earth, the Sun (God), and the cycle of life. All three musicians were concerned with the cycle of life; each explained his own version of the stages of this cycle, and the characteristics of each stage. They agreed that the drum was a communication system between the people and the creator, *Gichi Manitou*. The drum has the ability to draw people together. It is treated with respect, since the wooden frame is alive, and the hide membrane represents the animals who give their lives for us and from whom humans learn the meaning and value of sharing. All the musicians believed in the existence of and dichotomy between good and evil, variously represented as two roads or the world of light and the world of shadow. They stressed that we have the power to choose between the good (the path of respect, caring, and spiritual beliefs) and the bad (drugs, cheating, jealousy, and lack of spiritual beliefs).

In the new powwow-influenced Cree culture, the drum has returned but with different rules based on southern traditions. Before the drum can be played, it must be blessed by elders who place tobacco on its four sides. Before each powwow performance, a similar action is performed. One member of the drum group is chosen as the drum keeper, and I was told that "the way the drum sounds—it's the kind of person that individual is. It sounds rough, it sounds flat, then that person is crooked" (Azure 1981). The keeper cares for the drum, ensuring that it is never set directly on the ground, smudging it with sweetgrass to keep it purified, and offering tobacco to the drum spirits so that the singers will be strong. The drum, played with beaters, is set with the played side facing the sky. No menstruating women are allowed to touch it, and no one is allowed to play it casually. Besides blessing the new drum, the elders of the community instruct the young

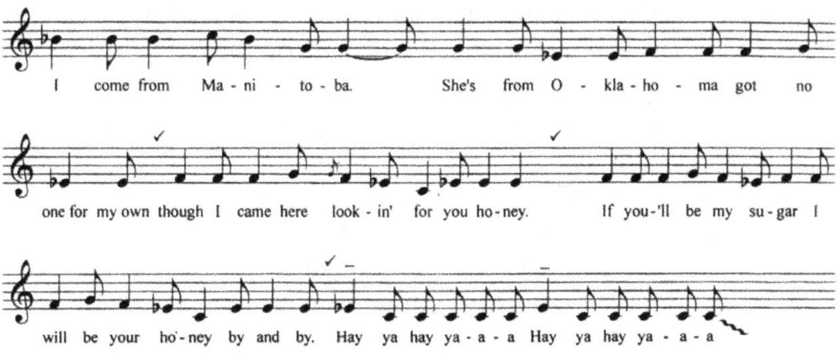

Figure 6.1: A 49er

group on their behaviour in relation to the sacred instrument. They must be respectful at all times toward the drum, which means no fighting, having only good feelings while around the drum, no drinking or drugs for four days before playing (to keep minds clear), and no consorting with menstruating women while at the powwow, since the women's power will interfere with the drummers' ability to sing. The names chosen for the drum group (and inscribed upon the drum) are symbolic of sacred objects such as a red sky or an eagle.

The drummers help control the progress of the powwow. Until they are seated, the dance cannot begin. The drums signify the start and finish of each dance, and are also frequently used as applause, to punctuate a joke or remark made by the MC. There are two main kinds of rhythms: ♩♩ for the main dance and ♩♪ for the social dances called *kahomeni* in Dakota, or 49ers. The 49ers begin late at night after the main powwow events are over. Young people gather informally to joke and make friends, and in the process many songs are generated for "funnin' around." The example in figure 6.1 is sung in the usual swinging compound rhythm (like "Row, row, row your boat"), but when the last line changes from English to syllables, the rhythm changes abruptly to simple duple time. Note also how the usual accents of the English language are altered, perhaps for humour, or perhaps the result of composing a song in a second language.

Round Dances

Musically and socially allied to the southern 49ers are the round dance songs. These are evening-long socials that continue to gain popularity across the North. Everyone can participate in these fun, informal dances and most anyone who has a hand drum can join the drum group. The form of the

songs is typical of Plains music: descending melodic phrases, the lead sings
out the tune, the group responds, the phrases continue to a melodically
level tail.

The basic dance pattern is a large circle in which people join hands and
step clockwise in time to the long–short beat of the hand drums. As the
dance progresses, the patterns become complex. People move around the
floor, joining hands and meeting new people. The dance, always drug-free,
is not only entertainment but also an opportunity to bring wellness and healing through social interaction. It is a sacred event in that the drums are
blessed and prayers are said to the Creator. Above all, the dance is about creating good feelings among the participants.

POWWOW SONG CHARACTERISTICS

Second only to the drum as a symbol of Indian identity is the tense, high-
pitched, warbling vocal production of the male powwow drummers, quite
different from the subarctic sound ideal discussed earlier. The scales are
built with few notes, often pentatonic. They are arranged as descending
melodies and sung with both words and vocables (patterned syllables) that
may have had semantic content in the past, and are rumoured to be meaningful now—a point that needs further study. Indeed, in at least one northern community, the people I spoke to believe that the songs composed of
syllables are the oldest, while songs in either Cree or English are newer.
Whatever their age and meaning, the syllables are more easily remembered
than words by those who do not speak an Aboriginal language. In addition,
singing with syllables enables Natives with different languages to join in
the songs.

Powwow songs are stable in form, congruent with Cree belief that many
of these songs come from the spirits in dreams, especially to medicine men.
This also fits anthropologist Bloch's thesis that formalization lends illocutionary force to ritual music (Bloch 1974, 73).[4] There are few variations of
this form. Each part has a specified religious meaning, so it is not manip-
ulated to serve individual desire for creativity. Moreover, entire powwow
songs are repeated many times: dances such as the Grand Entry, for instance,
require numerous repetitions of the song. After the announcer has calculated the number of participants and therefore the length of the Grand
Entry, he will direct the drummers to play accordingly, saying something
like, "Little brothers, Grand Entry, ten push-ups (repetitions)."

Figure 6.2 is a Cree drummer's diagram of his songs, followed by, in
figure 6.3, the author's notation of a northern Cree powwow song (Ed
Azure 1981).

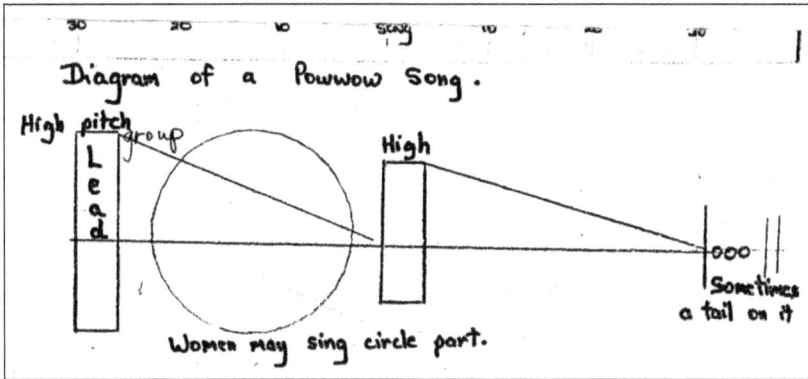

Figure 6.2: Cree drummer's diagram of powwow song

Figure 6.3: Music notation of a northern powwow song

Lead

The whole song is generally a spiritual song
This part here has a lot of spiritual significance
When the singers sing high it's a celebration of something
When they sing high, they're calling to those people
Who have departed from this earth
They're singing high so those people up there will hear them
Come on down. Come join us in our celebration

Group joins

And when they're singing here, they're singing to all the people all over
the world to come and join

High
Here, same thing again, high, again calling those people who have passed on

Tail
Some songs they'll put a tail on it
When they sing the tail they're sending acknowledgement
To creation in general
They're acknowledging creation; they're acknowledging earth
They're acknowledging God's work on earth
That's what a tail is for—thanking. (Azure 1981)

In addition, there is considerable reiteration of tones within the songs. Using musicologist Kolinski's method of music analysis (1982, 85), which is to compare the number of tone reiterations with the total number of progressions (arbitrarily set at one hundred) in a melody, I calculated fifty-nine as an average reiteration quotient of three powwow grass dance songs. For comparison, Kolinski prepared a chart that shows that the number of reiterations of tones is much higher in the religious songs of the Chippewa (sixty-five) than in their social songs (forty-eight). Such calculations support Bloch's thesis that repetition is an important quality of ritual music, and accounts for the fact that one singer can remember hundreds of these songs and learn new ones quickly, often within one or two hours. Thus, at several levels, repetition is a pervasive characteristic of powwow music. Repetition of the well-amplified songs immediately shows participants that this is a ritual, that sacralized time and space conditions have been created in which extraordinary power exists. Certainly, music in a context such as powwow is essential, not incidental.

Subarctic peoples respond wholeheartedly to the ritual aspect of powwow song. It has immediate and absolute power to enforce identity and is authoritative in a manner similar to the hunting songs and hymns. Many northern Cree now listen intently while others perform this music rooted in the plains. Although there may never be powwows on the scale of Plains events, subarctic drum groups receive regular invitations to perform at special community events such as the signing of an agreement with government. Today, powwow song can be heard in the commonly encountered sweat lodges and wherever a musical blessing is desired.

7

The Powwow: From the South to the Subarctic

When I pointed out to a northern friend how different powwow songs are from the old hunting songs, he replied that the Cree have been trading with Plains people since time immemorial, and that powwow may not be an entirely new sound in Canada's north. There is good evidence of a long-term Cree exposure to southern Native music. For example, neighbouring Algonquian speakers, the Ojibwe, received a large bass drum along with the Southern Dream Dance in Berens River, Manitoba, in the late 1800s.[1] Not only did the Cree trade with southerners, but also they travelled south to trade. Hudson's Bay Company records tell of a group of Cree hunters who left York Factory, Manitoba, on 23 August 1765 and journeyed south to the Riding Mountains (a direct distance of approximately 650 miles), hunting and trapping as they travelled. On 5 May 1766, they set out for the north again (Beaumont 1990, 14). Trips of this sort undoubtedly continued well into the next century, as long as European demand for furs made them worthwhile. So it is likely that some northern Cree heard Plains music, but so far there is no evidence to show they adopted any of it before the late twentieth century.

In fact, Plains powwow music in its present form would not have been heard in the eighteenth century, for it did not take its contemporary form until a century later; the modern powwow may have begun in Oklahoma during the armistice celebrations of 1918–19. William Powers states that the word *pauau*, of Algonquian origin, originally referred to a curing ceremony which might be attended by a great number of people (1971, 175). A brief history of powwow will show us how the powwow came to be, and finally, how it travelled to the north.

The origin of the powwow is in the grass or Omaha dance of the early 1800s. After the Omaha migrated west, their society was seriously weakened by disease and Sioux attacks.[2] One of their men's societies was joined with the Pawnee *Iruska* to form the *Hethushka* Society, later named the grass or Omaha dance. "The Omaha Dance was intended to stimulate an heroic spirit among the people and to keep alive the memory of historic and valorous acts" (Fletcher and La Flesche 1911, 459). In turn, the Omaha dance was taken up by the Yankton and then the Teton Sioux. The Dakota contributed their songs and not only elaborated upon the form but spread it across the northern plains. By the 1870s, the grass dance had reached many Plains peoples such as the Blackfeet, the Gros Ventre, the Hidatsa, the Crow, and the Piegan. In the 1880s, the Sarcee and the Bloods received the Grass Dance. It was observed among the northern Blackfoot in 1907, with the attendance of Sarcee and Cree visitors (Wissler 1913, 455). As the grass dance diffused, its sound changed. Orin T. Hatton writes that "the Teton contributed a strident quality to the vocal production and heavier pulsations on sustained tones.... From 1890 to the 1920s the Sioux dominated the Grass Dance. A northern style developed which was slower, introduced triplet rhythms in the vocal pulsations and a smooth falsetto vocal production for the introductory song phrases" (1986, 202). Hence the Sioux were instrumental in the spread and the sound of grass dance music.

Not only did the Sioux trade songs into Canada, but they also brought them after fleeing the violence in Minnesota in 1862. As refugees in Canada, the Dakota and other groups were impoverished, yet by exploiting all available resources they managed to survive, and historical sources show that they continued to dance. Fort Ellice journals indicate that when food was plentiful in the spring of 1872, they celebrated with a dance (Elias 1988, 226). In a letter written in 1907, Reverend John Thunder, a Presbyterian missionary at Oak Lake, objected to their dances and particularly the giveaways associated with them, which the non-Native population viewed as profligate (117). In 1884 or the following year, an agent complained that the Dakota spent much of the winter dancing and holding giveaways, giving much of their crop from a successful year to the neighbouring Cree (151).

Indian dancing was threatened in the south of Canada following the Indian Act of 1876. This act enabled the Canadian government to pass laws in the 1880s to suppress the Sun Dance with its giveaways. Other dances, such as the powwow, were viewed as less threatening to the non-Native establishment, and in most places, allowed to continue. But there were always conflicting views of the powwow. Indian agents and missionaries made strong recommendations that all powwows be stopped, whereas town councils promoted them for local fairs.

After 1955, the government dropped those portions of the Indian Act that forbade all Indian dances, and since that time the events have increased in size and frequency. One of the first large inter-tribal powwows in Manitoba occurred in 1970, sponsored by the Manitoba Indian Brotherhood and widely publicized as Manitoba Indian Days. A decade later, small pow-wow events were occurring in northern Manitoba as well.

Continual exchanges with more southerly groups such as the Ojibwe are implicit in the spread of the powwow. One young Cree person, influenced by an Ojibwe man, was among the first to actively teach the powwow in northern Manitoba. His contribution is discussed in the next section.

The Way He Walked Was Different

Ed Azure grew up along the bayline, which was the name given to the railway dotted with train stops running between Winnipeg and Hudson Bay. He attended a non-Native elementary school and then a Roman Catholic day school. He remembers trying to sneak out of both. His childhood was happy because he had opportunity to play freely in the bush and he was cared for by family and relatives. He was unaware of Native culture until one day when a young Ojibwe man came to the reservation near the town of The Pas, Manitoba, to marry a Cree girl. A small fellow, the man walked with a straight back and his chest out. Ed's first reaction was hostile, but soon he realized there was something about the man that made Ed feel good, because "the way he walked was different" (Azure 1981).

Eventually they talked, and Ed took his first steps on the "Indian Road." In 1970, through talking with this man, Ed began to learn about various aspects of Native culture in other parts of Canada. His interest in this led to his attending a powwow in Winnipeg, Manitoba. He wasn't overly impressed, but at least the experience showed him what powwows were. Soon afterwards, he and some friends heard about a caravan going across the country in preparation for a Native youth conference. They jumped into a rented van to join the others in Cornwall, Ontario. Later, in Ottawa, they were able to secure a small grant, approximately two thousand dollars, which helped them to form a cultural group. They bought feathers and other needed items to make dancing outfits, and Ed was delegated to make the long journey from The Pas to Winnipeg to buy a large Ludwig bass drum.

His time in Ottawa and Winnipeg left him surprised at the strength of the cultural awareness of city dwellers; he felt that northerners had a lot to learn. Indeed, the Ojibwe teacher's role in The Pas has become Ed's role in the neighbouring city of Thompson, Manitoba, a town originally built around nickel mines in the 1950s. Thompson's origins in mining resulted in plenty of available housing, which has been gradually taken over by the original residents of the area, the Cree.

Ed's teaching style, which is aimed at developing ideas about Native identity in his community, reflects his Cree personality. His disavowal of absolute leadership is not unusual in a hunting society, which, outside of the immediate family, was traditionally leaderless. Like most Cree, he does not like to impose his will on others; each person he works with, even the very young, is recognized as self-reliant and given room to make choices.

Ed believes that it is important to live quietly and set a good example. "You can go around with lots of words, but actions count," he told me. "That's what they're watching" (Azure 1981). He feels "that Native people are just sitting back and watching to see how traditional culture will go. They're not even asking questions, just waiting." Meanwhile, it is important to Ed to live a life of the mind—the simple Cree way, with truth and kindness as the watchwords, depending as little as possible on technological gadgetry.

Many of Ed's first efforts centred on the local Red Sky group, called this because the old people viewed a red sky in the evening as the harbinger of a beautiful dawn. The focus was on raising consciousness in both Native and non-Native people concerning Native spirituality, but there was disagreement about the meaning of "traditional culture." Ed Azure has developed his own definition:

> It is a system of ideas and a philosophy that has taken form through such things as conferences, Native awareness, education in the schools. [It is used for] courses in the universities, powwows, and celebrations, and in educating the public at large, as well as Indian people themselves, in Native cultural and spiritual awareness. (Azure 1981)

Likewise, Ed was convinced of the importance of spirituality, and he took action to learn himself and then to teach others. He travelled to neighbouring provinces when his own elders would not help.

In a presentation to undergraduate students in 1981, Ed said: "Generally Indian music, the important part, is what the songs symbolize, mean. The underneath stuff is very important. That's what makes everything fit together." He stressed the commonality of the human condition, stating that within Indian culture there is a way of life for everyone. He gave the Boy Scout movement in Thompson as an example of whites espousing Indian qualities. Ed has helped the Scouts, and endorses their choice of lifestyle and code of ethics. After singing "The Red Sky Song," one of the first songs he learned, Ed said, "That's Indian music," then continued, "but I am really questioning that now. Seeing as how everybody had drums at one time, maybe we all sang that way or similar." He pointed out that all Native cultures still use the pipes, the rattle, the drum, and also braid their hair. Later, he repeated that all societies have a drum, but Native people have retained knowledge of how it is to be used. To the Native, the drum, braids, pipe, and rattle have retained their sacredness. Ed described the rattle, in a new addition to his teachings, as representing the mind, God's greatest gift to humankind, and mentioned that before contact with whites, the old people communicated mind-to-mind.

The drum is central to his teaching. Ed pointed out the different kinds of drums, with names such as "community," "ceremonial," "hand," and "water." As Ed began removing the blanket from the large bass drum, a student asked to whom the drum belonged. Ed's response was that he wasn't sure but that usually a drum has a drum keeper who ensures that the drum is wrapped at all times. There is a special case for the sticks, and a little pouch on the side of the drum filled with sweetgrass or with a throat medicine that the drummer uses for singing. When the drum-keeper takes the drum out, the singers and the sticks are ceremonially smudged with sweetgrass. An offering is given by putting tobacco on the four corners of the drum. The four corners represent the four qualities of caring, feeling, relationships, and respect. As mentioned earlier, children are not allowed to play with it, nor menstruating women to go near it. The way it sounds is a reflection of the kind of person that the drummer is.

In 1981, Ed organized a Native Awareness week in Thompson, Manitoba, designed specifically to instruct people in Native culture.[3] The week concluded with an indoor powwow (because January temperatures in Thompson are constantly below freezing) in a large hall adjoining the local Ukrainian church. It featured dancing and feasting and the traditional giveaways.

The powwow, which had been open to the entire population of Thompson, free of charge, was apparently a huge success in the eyes of Thompson's Native community, which went on to organize an outdoor powwow later that year, assisted by various local Native organizations. This event was larger and the attendees were from various social groups—though almost all were local Cree—resulting in less closeness than at the earlier powwow. The singers, dancers, and bright outfits were too distanced from the audience, making it an attraction for the curious but not a mode of expression for the devotee (see figs. 7.1 and 7.2). However, the powwow certainly caused both the Native and non-Native onlookers to consider this culture a real and active force in this northern city.

Powwow history is shaped by individuals such as Ed Azure. The ideas and ideals of powwow are transmitted personally by such people using

Figures 7.1 and 7.2: Photographs of a demonstration powwow in Thompson, MB, 1981

song, dance, and drum. They see a great need in the Cree community for a heritage; they hope that a stronger sense of identity will alleviate alcoholism and build stronger individuals and societies. And, in contrast to the prohibitions of the Indian Act mentioned earlier, the Canadian government began to support Aboriginal cultural initiatives during the last decades of the twentieth century. Clearly, powwows have been an important part and carrier of the Native message and, while the sounds were foreign at first, over the past few decades they have become commonplace in the subarctic.

Powwow: The Popular Music for the Native American

The powwow is an ideal subject for tracing changes in Native music. In just over a century, the northern Plains peoples such as the Dakotas, Bloods, and Assiniboines have witnessed the dissolution of many of their traditional tribal ceremonies, the creation of an inter-tribal powwow, and, as we have just read, the spread of their music and teachings into Canada's north and beyond. Within the last three decades, powwow music has become a globally recognized art form performed at world gatherings from Europe to Australia.

In this twenty-first century, culture and language loss continues apace for the northern Cree, and the powwow, as a system of Native belief, is becoming entrenched. Powwow offers the possibility to seek out an Indian spiritual life; the beliefs are actively espoused and taught by the new generation of northern elders. There are drum groups in many of the communities, and generalized Native Studies is taught in schools.

Although the powwow adherents are more certain about how to proceed in carving out an Indian identity, they remain limited in number in the subarctic because, as elsewhere, there is a plethora of choice. While country music remains ubiquitous, my students now list other music as favourites, such as reggae or the blues, even *The Three Tenors*. Aboriginal northerners are part of the world music community, and some now have musical tastes more in common with urban dwellers than with others on their reserves. The pre-media world of small human groupings bound together by oral traditions has given way to the various groupings made possible by the expansion of the media.

Powwow song has been referred to as the popular music of the Indian world. For the past three decades the songs have been spread across North America by tape cassettes, informally recorded by standing near the drum groups as they play. Now digital format is common, mostly video, and more and more drum groups are making and marketing recordings professionally. A few remote communities have privately owned digital recording studios where local groups can record their songs. There is evidence that powwow is joining mainstream North American music. For example, the tempos of powwow songs are close to those of popular music. Indeed, several of my young students have told me they practise their powwow dancing at home to rock music. I have even heard "49ers" accompanied by electric guitar and rock drums instead of the usual hand drum.

Powwow songs are becoming well bounded with clearly defined beginnings and endings, as is the case with non-Native compositions. In the past, song beginnings were "slow," that is, individual musicians tapped their drums lightly and hummed until a consensus regarding song choice, pitch, and speed was reached and the group burst into full song. This practice still occurs, but infrequently, because competing powwow drum groups wish to present a polished performance, as do powwow musicians making studio recordings. Drum groups, although mostly Cree in the North, may be truly inter-tribal and the use of English words and vocables allows any music-lover to join. Names of the dances are changing too: traditionally, powwow songs were named to indicate the appropriate dance, such as "Intertribal Dance," "Grand Entry," and so on. Now, like any popular tune, they are given catchy names such as "Pure Playaz," "Luneez," and "Phenomenon."[4]

To what extent have these developments in powwow music occurred among subarctic Cree people? For the moment, the popular-cultural effects are certainly muted, and the people largely restrict the powwow songs to community ceremonial contexts. Like the hunting songs, the music is treated with reverence and its primary purpose remains spiritual communication. Tony Seeger's statement about South American indigenous peoples applies equally to the northern Cree: "Our assumption that music is an 'art,' a primarily aesthetic and therefore incidental activity, has led us astray.... To these societies music is a fundamental part of social life, not merely one of its options" (1979, 392).

Conclusion

Remarkable in this history is the observable change in performed music, within three decades, from hunting songs to powwow music. Until the 1970s, for most northern Cree, music *was* hunting songs, hymns, and fiddle tunes, fashioned over the centuries from the rhythms of the subarctic landscape to fit Cree personality. The Cree hunters sang songs reflecting the rhythms of nature, especially those of the animals they hunted.

Before the Euro-Canadians arrived, animals were viewed as benefactors: humankind was dependent upon their willingness to be sacrificed. If moose were encountered, it was believed that they had given themselves, and all would be slaughtered. Proper ritual ensured that the animals would repeatedly and willingly give themselves to be slain. The current view of conservation, made necessary by the killing of more animals than nutritionally necessary, was not held by subsistence hunters, nor was it needed.

Over time, trapping changed this covenant with the animals. Guns, better traps, and bait, such as castoreum for the beaver, made the hunters more effective and led to game shortages, such as those experienced in northern Manitoba in the late eighteenth century, when fur-bearing animals were severely depleted. In view of the endurance of hunting, historians have tended to gloss over the different ideologies required for hunting and trapping animals, but the songs embedded in the hunt show that three centuries of involvement in the fur trade, from the proto-contact period around 1682 to the present, wrought enormous change to the Cree ethos.[1]

Animals were no longer seen as physical manifestations of spirits, but as objects whose numbers could be controlled by humans. Hunting became an increasingly aggressive rather than pacific endeavour; proper thought and proper songs were no longer primary strategies for bringing the animals to the hunter. By the 1930s, the cause of game depletion was understood by the Cree not to be the result of improper religious rites but the result of overhunting. By the 1940s, traplines were introduced into Manitoba. In northern Quebec, the development of family territories and usufructuary

rights led to animal management. Some hunters began conservation meas-
ures, such as leaving a few beavers in the lodge, sparing juvenile moose
and caribou, and allowing the land to "rest" periodically by not hunting on
it. In 1982, in Wemindji, Quebec, hunter Harry Hughboy told me,

> My father would tell us to stop hunting while it was still day
> because my father wanted to be careful how many birds he hunted
> My father was always careful how much game he hunted
> He taught me the lesson only to hunt what I need
> because if I over-hunt I will pay for it in the end
> I will not be able to survive.

In addition, despite Hudson's Bay Company pressure on the Cree to
hunt and trap, the old primary strategy for capturing animals—mobility—
was gradually abandoned in favour of sedentism. Initially, the Cree tended
to stay longer and longer at the posts: some, as stated earlier, became
"homeguard Indians." Later, if they wanted their children educated in
western style, they were anchored to the community for much of the year.
Reliance on food preservation increased; families who no longer moved
with the animal populations were distanced, not only physically, but also
psychologically from those animals.

Moreover, Hudson's Bay Company personnel assisted with medicine
as well as food. Niezen writes, "Alan Nicholson, the post manager at Rupert's
House (now Waskaganish) at the turn of the century, is described in a fur
trader's autobiography as the community's principal healer" (1997, 470).
In 1837, the Hudson's Bay Company's charter was renewed on condition
that it "improve" the Native people's spiritual lives (Long 1986, 314), which
meant that more missionaries arrived; they offered supplemental food and
rudimentary health care. Finally, when the federal government introduced
transfer payments, dependence upon the goodwill of animals was over.
Indeed, in several narratives, elders jokingly referred to the animals as
money: "I'm tearing the paper, I'm paying the bills with the fox as I kill"
(Lameboy, Song 62).

Western health care was indeed a blow to the continuance of Cree song.
In the 1980s, I recorded no songs about healing plants, yet the Cree, like
other Native groups, had long used plants for this purpose. (For example,
in the early twentieth century, Frances Densmore studied the healing plants
and songs of the Chippewa, who speak an Algonquian language as do the
Cree.) George Nelson wrote of the northern Cree of Lac la Ronge in 1823:

> As far as I can learn, every different root, herb, plant, mineral, Spirit (or
> whatever you may please to term this latter) have each their respective

songs, and which they must sing, were his voice like that of a choked Pig, when he employs them for one of themselves, or learns them to another. When they sing, those of their familiars who instructed this Song, whether to the one who sings, as having learnt it from himself (i.e., familiar) or having been handed to him; he is said to attend, invisibly, of course, and perform that which he promised this (medecine, supposing it is one) should effect. (Brown and Brightman 1988, 59)

And Samson Lameboy of Chisasibi recalled:

A long time ago we never had any medicine
We produced our own, for cuts
That's all gone now, nobody has written about it. (1984)

Healers who used the songs and plants were delegitimized by the epidemics caused by European pathogens, and much knowledge was lost through the untimely deaths from disease of knowledgeable persons. Cree healers were not equipped to treat diseases such as influenza and measles, and more and more they sought the help of outsiders. Federal government initiatives in health care rendered local practices superfluous, and local health practices, such as midwifery, were given little place. The Cree were strongly encouraged to cooperate with often paternalistic health-care workers.

Now, health care is mainly in the hands of outsiders who operate according to models standardized throughout the developing world. In 1950, a hospital with thirty-two beds was opened in Fort George (Chisasibi) to treat the great numbers sick with tuberculosis, an illness exacerbated by crowded and poor housing. As a result of the land claims settlement with the province of Quebec in 1975, services have expanded through the establishment of the Cree Regional Board of Health and Social Services (CRBHSS). However, as Richard Salisbury pointed out in 1986, "The CRBHSS has not advanced as far as the CSB (Cree School Board) in the process of adapting to become part of Cree society. All the eight physicians and professionals are non-Cree, as are all the registered nurses in the hospital, and half of the administrative staff" (68).

Niezen sums it up well: "Changes to Cree culture were encouraged not through moral imperatives but through technological promises and legal sanctions. The health care of the Cree became assimilated into a formal juridical system beyond their control" (1997, 478). Shamanic healing with dreams, songs, and herbology was mightily challenged, although in recent years it has experienced a revival.

The healing songs and hunting songs evoked the Cree identity shaped over centuries, whereas hymns and country music instructed them in a new order. From country music they learned the non-Native concept that human relationships, especially romantic love, are primary in the natural order, and from both they learned the English language. Initially, country music, like the Christian hymns, was subject to modification of language, rhythm, and content to fit the Cree ethos, but media transmission inundated the local culture too quickly with too much new music for a distinctly Cree country music to survive.

So far, the subarctic Cree have not altered the sound of powwow music in the way they initially changed other received musics. Media technology has fostered powwow growth, and it has been an effective tool for proclaiming Native identity, reaching, as we have seen, into isolated parts of northern Canada. But the Cree hunting songs are gone and their replacement, Plains Indian music, a conscious choice for many, is a musical affirmation for modernism. In 1965, Canadian philosopher George Grant presaged events this way: "Modern civilization makes all local cultures anachronistic" (54). Now, the joyous musically and textually creative songs in the Algonquian language are seldom sung. One often hears regret expressed for a person's inability to speak Cree or to speak it well, whereas in the 1980s it was common to hear an elder say, "I love speaking Cree." Natives understood the homologies among humans, animals, and plants necessary for survival. To catch a wild animal, they had to "listen" to the patterns and dictates of nature. In a way not yet fully understood, song could be an instrument of their will. We do know that songs helped the hunters to focus their thoughts and energize their bodies to prepare for the hunt. And we do know that while there was no expressed aesthetic of music, the Cree took great pleasure in creating their miniature portraits of animals in clever verse set to song.

Cree hunting song suggests the complexity of the natural environment. The singer may begin anywhere and end at any time, and although the overall patterning of phrases is constant, both the pitch and length of the notes are slightly changed with each repetition to fit the words. Furthermore, the solo singer can vary the notes as wished, depending upon the singer's mood and the audience. As we have seen, Cree singers do exactly this, so that even the old hymns begin to sound like traditional Cree song. Ken Blacksmith of Waskaganish said, "Most of the hymns become a chant" (2002).

In contrast, western music is built upon chords, undoubtedly resulting from indoor performance. Chords indicate a shift in worldview, because their premise is forward movement. Chords build tension to a climax; they drive the song to its end. Chords also require precise timing. If three or four moving parts are to be sounded simultaneously, there must be agreement among the performers as to tempo, breathing spots, and other pauses. Thus western music has regularly recurring divisions or metres of three or four patterns, readily felt in a waltz or march. Harmony— patterns of chords—is a strong organizer of time and produces a different music from the rhythmically flexible and individualistic Cree approach to song.

Cree knowledge was not the temporary, cerebral knowledge of the urban dweller, of the institutionally educated. Theirs was a deep understanding of their environment and their place in this environment, acquired through countless generations of adaptation. The fact that in North America there are identifiable traditional musics coterminous with geographic areas suggests that the diversity of human musics stems from long exposure to the different sounds of the physical environments in which the makers are rooted.

Technology has allowed us to insulate ourselves from the potential of our innate understanding of the natural world. To catch a wild animal, the hunter had to anticipate its thoughts and learn its habitat. What we have gained in comfort, we have lost in ingenuity and the ability to tap into the wisdom inherited from our ancestors. Old Cree song is an outpouring of this wisdom both in structure and function.

Before modern media, song did not live apart from a human carrier. The Native population had song and a sense of self, but little means to extend either artificially. It was not practicable for a hunting society to acquire goods, land, nor material icons of their songs. Mind and memory carried almost everything. Perhaps this explains the strong attachment of individuals to their songs: the ideas were carried in their minds, never preserved on a plastic object such as an audiotape. Further, memories had value for corporeal survival and were not carelessly erased or exchanged. In contrast, non-Natives are able to create the illusion of permanence. They have devised a multitude of ways to hold the potentiality of sound—hard disc, CD, cassette tape, notation on paper.

The one pronounced thread of continuity in Native music, however, has been its grounding in oral tradition. The learning of music, from the hunting to powwow songs, has been by listening, followed by imitation. This process continues, greatly facilitated by technology. During the last several decades, much listening, particularly to powwow music, has involved playing cassette tapes and, more recently, using digital formats. This change has greatly accelerated inter-tribal exchange and loss of ceremonial contexts. Recording also dictates changes in the aesthetics of powwow music, for recording technology has requirements to do with the length of performances, clarity, timing, and percussion/vocal balance.

Thus, while recording machines facilitate song exchange and probably enable larger individual repertoires across the continent, they also result in reduced need for involvement in the social event itself, thereby diminishing the performance context. It seems to me that the greatly accelerated exchange of songs across the continent has led to music "levelling" as well.

The past century was a time of personal turmoil for the Cree. They did not fit in the non-Native world, nor could they still live in hunting societies. The values still prevalent among northern Natives make it difficult for them to succeed in ways that non-Natives recognize and approve. One might think that the non-acquisitive outlook of northern people would be greatly appreciated on our crowded planet!

The arrival of powwow in the North is due partly to the efforts of a few people who despaired at the tragedies resulting from cultural disintegration. They deliberately chose the new identity found in pan-Indian teachings. Powwow is not a gradual change to the local music; it is a new music borrowed from the outside. At present, powwow music and teachings have gained a firm hold across the North and have become essential to many Cree for the renewal of their identity and psychological health. Gospel music, too, fulfills the northern Cree predilection for a spiritual context for their music.

However, as for all citizens of the twenty-first century, these are only a few of the many ways to express oneself musically and to view the world. Many young northerners have chosen to become "modern" in the broader North American sense. Native youth feel free to choose a music and an identity, unlike their grandparents and often parents, who, rooted in a particular physical environment, had little choice in matters of lifestyle and music.

Still, more and more Cree are looking to their own heritage for inspiration. They incorporate into their songs their stories and language, music instruments such as rattles and drums, and even local sounds. And, as you have read, the Cree do have a musical heritage of hunting songs that are unique both in sound and function. These oral expressions are an invaluable example of human diversity and of the seamless fit of a people with their natural environment. The Cree want to know their history, and this account of music change over three decades is but one small part of the story upon which to build.

Afterword

In *Essential Song*, Lynn Whidden has given us an example of indigenous music from the northeastern subarctic Cree community of Chisasibi, Quebec. Whidden describes and interprets the hunting songs she has collected and their importance in the spiritual, emotional, and psychological world of Cree hunters. Whidden shows how hunting songs connected hunters to their hunting spirits and to the animals they loved and hunted. Indeed, this is a very different understanding of hunting in which animals participate with hunters in the hunt and give themselves to conscientious hunters who act appropriately in respecting the protocols that sustain animals.

In the 1980s, hunting songs were becoming something of a memory for the Cree Elders of Chisasibi who still carried the knowledge and occasionally performed their hunting songs within community life. Sadly, the Elders felt that contemporary Cree generations did not know the hunting songs' ceremonial, spiritual, and religious importance. Similarly, in my youth as a Cree boy growing up in Moose Factory, Ontario, I did not know the hunting traditions and songs of our people or even that they existed. Although my family environment consisted of Cree language, food, and stories, what I knew of "being Indian" was very different and removed in many aspects from those of my ancestors who practised the old ways.

One day, in the early 1970s, I happened upon my father (an ordained Cree Anglican minister) listening to strange singing coming from his reel-to-reel tape recorder. This strange voice sounded like moaning, but my father explained that it was a Cree person singing a song from Eastmain, Quebec. To me it sounded as foreign as Moroccan drum music. I thought of the singing as something "Indian" and perhaps old, from the "bush" Indians whom I considered different from us. I had no idea that what I was hearing was from a hunting culture and tradition that my family, parents, grandmother, and I were directly descended from.

In my adulthood, like many contemporary Cree, I have become interested in the language, traditions, oral stories, and music of our people.

Hunting songs have become a part of my quest for knowledge and insight into an important Cree style of human expression. Like the desires of the Cree Elders of Chisasibi (1980s) in having their hunting song traditions passed down to future generations, Lynn Whidden's work in a very significant way has enabled this process to continue. Her book documents the elders' knowledge and communicates it so that it can be passed on to individuals such as myself and other future Cree peoples. Moreover, the elders' knowledge via Whidden's book has tremendously expanded my understanding, knowledge, and interpretation of hunting songs.

Essential Song bridges a gap between the Cree Elders of Chisasibi and contemporary Crees wishing to understand the hunting "tool" complex, hunting philosophy, and animal spirituality of their ancestors who were so deeply connected to the land and animals. The elders also show us that, as contemporary Crees, we continue to need the land and animals in sharing our stories of the past, but most importantly, in building a strong sense of ourselves with new, oral futures. Indeed, for contemporary Cree musicians like myself, Whidden's book provides a window into the past and a departure point for incorporating hunting songs into annual Cree festivals and community gatherings. Perhaps the hunting songs can be used as tools again, this time for building understanding of, and respect for, the religious aspects of the music, hunting culture, and animal spirituality of our ancestors.

Stanley L. Louttit, M.A.
Independent Cree writer/researcher
Wemindji, QC

Appendix I

Frequently Sung Hymns in Chisasibi, Quebec

COMPILED BY REVEREND LOCKE

I include the following list shared with me by Reverend Wetmore (see chap. 4) to show the hymns favoured by the Cree in 1982. Each hymn was written in Cree in phonetic syllables, English words, and syllabics. The main sources of these hymns, both tunes and words, are the Church of England *Book of Common Prayer* (1905, 1938 editions) and Ira Sankey's *Sacred Songs and Solos*.

Regular Service

Holy, Holy, Holy
Awake My Soul
Sun of My Soul
Now the Day Is Over (tune)
How Sweet the Hour
Soldiers of the Cross Arise

The Advent of Our King
Glory to Thee
By Cool Siloam (tune)
God from on High Hath Heard
Sweet Savior Bless Us Ere We Go
Great God What Do I See and Hear

Advent

There Is a Happy Land
   (sometimes sung to the tune of
   "Nearer My God to Thee")
Lo He Comes with Clouds Ascending
Hark the Glad Sound
Christians Awake
O Come All Ye Faithful
Hark the Herald Angels Sing
Angels from the Same Realms of Glory
Souls of Men (New Year Hymn)
A Few More Years (New Year)
As with Gladness, Men of Old

Hark a Herald Voice
Thy Kingdom Come O Lord
Thou Whose Almighty Lord
Angels from the Realm
God Be with You
O God Unseen
O Thou Who Makest
At Even When the Sun Is Set
O Christ Thou Hast Ascended
Nearer My God to Thee
Resting from His Work Today

Good Friday

The Church's One Foundation
Three in One and One in Five
Now My Tongue the Mystery Telling

O Thou Who Makest
Sinful Sighing to Be Blest

Lent

Alas and Did My Saviour Bleed
Jerusalem on High (Easter Day)
O Zion Open Wide Thy Gates
Sinful Sighing to Be Blest
O the Bitter Shame
Abide with Me
Lead Kindly Light
Jesus Calls Us
Jesus the Very Thought of Thee
Lord Dismiss Us

Come Holy Ghost, Descend from High
Jesus Christ Is Risen Today
Lord Behold Us with Thy Favour
Forever with the Lord
Jesus Lover of My Soul
Upon the Holy Mount
Those Eternal Bowers
Jerusalem on High
Who Are Those Like Saints Appearing
Forever with the Lord

Easter

Awake Awake O Christians
Our Blest Redeemer
My God and Is Thy Table Spread

Three in One and One in Three
This Is the Day of Light
Sinful Sighing to Be Blest

Ascension

I Hunger and I Thirst
Till He Come O Let the Word

Not Worthy Lord
The Lord's My Shepherd

Baptism

By Cool Siloam

Wedding

Stand Up Stand Up for Jesus
Brightly Gleams Our Banner
Onward Christian Soldiers
Lead Us Heavenly Father

Saviour Again to Thy Dear Name
I Will Guide Thee
O Thou Who Makest Souls to Shine

Confirmation

I Am but a Stranger Here
Saviour Again to Thy Dear Name
Jesus I Have Promised
The Lord's My Shepherd
Have Mercy on Us God Most High
The Highest and the Holiest Place
Do No Sinful Action
Jesus Loves Me
Through the Love of God Our Saviour
O God Our Help (to the tune of God
    Save the Queen)

Ride On, Ride On
Come Ye Thankful People Come
Alleluia Sing to Jesus
Now Thank We All Our God
All People That on Earth
To Thy Temple
Come Unto Me Ye Weary
I Heard the Voice

Funeral

Be Thou My Guardian
Tell Me the Old Old Story
While Shepherds Watched
Praise to God Immortal Praise
The Church's One Foundation
Ride On, Ride On
This Is the Day of Light
Come Labour On
To the Work!
There Is a Gate
Wondrous Love
Fear Not, God Is Thy Shield
Come
Saviour Lead Me Lest I Stray
Look and Live
Bless Me Now
Pass Me Not O Gentle Saviour
O There Is Pardon for You
At the Cross
The Great Physician
What a Friend We Have in Jesus
Glad and Glorious Gospel
Jesus My Saviour
Down in the Valley
Christ Receiveth Sinful Men
All People That on Earth (doxology)
All People That on Earth
  (grace for meals)
Awake Awake
Whiter Than Snow
Let the Sunshine In
Be Loyal to Jesus
Hold the Fort
There Is Life
There Is a Happy Land
Sweet Bye and Bye

Safe in the Arms of Jesus
Jesus of Nazareth Passeth By
How Vain the Cruel Herod
I Am So Glad That Jesus Loves Me
Dare to Be a Daniel
Jesus Is Calling
All to Jesus I Surrender
Only an Armor-Bearer
I've Found a Friend
Who Is on the Lord's Side
It Is Well
Glory for Me
When the Roll Is Called Up Yonder
The Lifeboat
Count Your Blessings
Gospel Bells
Fully Trusting
What a Gathering
Have You Been to Jesus
Jesus Saviour Pilot Me
Eternal Father Strong to Save
Praise Ye the Lord
Let Us Hear You Tell It
Hear the Call
The Crowning Day
The Coming of the Kingdom
I Am Praying for You
Love Lifted Me
I Am Happy to Follow Jesus
Jesus Shall Reign
God Sees the Little Sparrow Fall
I'll Be a Sunbeam
O Canada
God Save the Queen
Silent Night

Appendix II

The Eighty-Six Songs, with Topics and Commentary,
of the 1982 and 1984 Collections
(original recordings in the Canadian Museum of Civilization)

1
Performer: William Jack
Topic: goose

This is a song about a goose. I am calling them to come near so I can kill them. I sang it after I got married because I was happy [joke] and when hunting. I learned this song from my grandfather a long time ago.

Interpreter's comments:
"Here he lands; here they are very close." It has other words but I can't understand them.

2 (CD track 1)
Performer: William Jack
Topic: fox

I used to love going fox-hunting.
I saw a fox very well built, a healthy fox.
He was orange; he had an orange-brown back.
I went to check out my traps to see if the orange-back was there.
He was caught in my trap, the orange-back.
I sang this song when I started out hunting in the morning.

Interpreter's comments:
In the song he repeats the colour of the fox.

3 (CD track 2)
Performer: William Jack
Topic: beaver

I am going to sing about the beaver.
I didn't kill beaver too often but still I am going to sing about the beaver.
But I killed a lot of foxes.
I sing about how the beaver keeps his food under water.
How the trees float down the water because of the beaver.

I sing it before I start to hunt in the morning and any time when I want to sing, when I am happy.

4 (CD track 3)
Performer: William Jack
Topic: lake trout
> I'm going to sing about the lake trout.
> That's it! A very short song

5 (CD track 4)
Performer: William Jack
Topic: rabbit
> I'm going to sing about the rabbit.
> You probably didn't hear about the rabbit.
> That's the bowels of the rabbit.
> Take that and rub it against the sinew.
> We used to say we're going to laugh at the rabbit
> Because he's going to eat his own insides.

6 (CD track 5)
Performer: William Jack
Topic: the seagull
> It is a funny song. I was a guide with my son who speaks English. The white-men always had tape recorders and wanted me to sing or tell stories. And I saw this seagull flying along searching for food. Then I said to my son, "They always make me sing songs or tell stories. Here's the song I'm going to tell him because white people eat seagulls."
> The seagull, the seagull, the seagull.
> That eats, eats and eats the whiteman.
> That's the one who always eats the whiteman

Interpreter's comments:
We natives don't eat seagulls—they're junk eaters. William Jack turned the song around—the seagull ate the whitemen. Like many of the songs the Native people sing: they turn them around.

7 (CD track 6)
Performer: William Jack
Topic: winterbird
> I'm going to sing about the winterbird.
> Somebody was thinking as he was walking with his snowshoes.
> The person was thinking, I wish I could fly.
> Then he suddenly remembered the winterbird.
> He was very fast with his snowshoes.
> He was so fast that he thought he was flying like a winterbird.
> Then he thought he would steal the song of the winterbird.

8

Performer: George Pepabano

Topic: otter

> I was singing about an otter, the fur of an otter.
> An otter song from long ago.
>
> *Interpreter's comments:*
>> It is looking at me (*repeats four times*).
>> The otter, the otter fur.
> I can't get words at the end of the song

9

George Pepabano

Topic: hunting (ducks, deer)

> Now I'm going to sing a hunting song.
> This is how the song goes.
> I am singing about making ducks [decoys].
> It was in the water, then the deer came along.

10

Performer: George Pepabano

Topic: beaver

> People used to sing different songs.
> They sang about almost anything that they hunted.
> Now here's a beaver song.
> The person feels like the beaver is going so fast that it feels like tin rattling.
> The person who made up the song said
> It feels like the beaver just came out of this place.
> When he went out to kill the beaver
> It just came out in front of him.
> My father's grandfather didn't use guns when hunting.

11

Performer: George Pepabano

Topic: snowshoes and young hunter

> Now I'm going to sing about snowshoes.
> This is a young man who is now a hunter.
> And the deer was talking to him in the shaking tent.
> It's about the young hunter just starting out his hunting
> And he's having a conversation with the deer.
> He puts on his new snowshoes and all his hunting gear
> And goes out to get the deer.
> You know when we're telling legends.
> Legends go from mouth to mouth and person to person.
> If the legend is being passed down from person to person it changes,
> But the old songs still have their main theme

And their main characters intact, they don't really change.
The old songs that are passed by generations.

Interpreter's comments:
This is not really his song; this is a song that has passed down. He's singing
about the snowshoes first, then he switches over to the young hunter.

12
Performer: George Pepabano
Topic: porcupine
> I'm going to sing about a porcupine.
> There's a tall tree with the porcupine
> Climbing it to the top.

13 (CD track 7)
Performer: George Pepabano
Topic: partridge
> This song is about the partridge bird.
> The partridge, and how he runs through the snow.
> His feet are able to carry him through the snow on top, without sinking.
> The hunter compares himself to this bird, to a partridge.
> When he has on his snowshoes he is able to run
> Like the partridge on top of the snow.

14 (CD track 8)
Performer: George Pepabano
Topic: man and bear
> I'm going to sing about the bear.
> It's about this man who lives with a bear.
> The bear lives off berries.
> The man asks the bear for some berries.
> It's about the man and the bear

15
Performer: George Pepabano
Topic: mountain and poor man
> This song is about a big mountain.
> Right near the mountain are nice big beautiful fish.
> It's about a certain individual who was very poor.
> It was his first time to kill, to bring home his first hunt.
> But something was looking after him while he was poor.

16
Performer: George Pepabano
Topic: young man sings about his father, who had supernatural powers
> This is a song about a young man singing about his father
> Who had supernatural powers through the shaking tent.

The young man had the same thing too, so he's singing about it.
They both had powers, that is how they communicate with each other.

17
Performer: George Pepabano
Topic: young hunter who kills deer by using the shaking tent
This is about a deer, a deer song.
The song is about a young hunter and his knowledge of the shaking tent;
How he can kill the deer through using the shaking tent.

18 (CD track 9)
Performer: George Pepabano
Topic: making a canoe/loon
This is a song that my father used to sing
When he went in his canoe to look for geese.
He made the canoe and he was very skilful in making the canoe
Out of birchbark and the roots from the tree.
He was very skilful in hunting for the goose.
My father made the canoe and he was very skilful.

19
Performer: George Pepabano
Topic: the white man
I understand that you don't really know the old Cree language.
The ancient kind of Cree, very poetic, from long ago.
I know you young people don't understand it now.
Because you speak English and a bit of French,
You begin to lose your language.
But for me, I know you young people mix English and Cree together.
You don't try to speak all Cree, that's why you're losing it.
You should try to speak all Cree.
Long ago when the government came in, made contact,
They were going to teach me how to speak English.
They never got around to it, but it doesn't matter anymore.
I love to speak Cree.
This song is about the whiteman,
The traces he leaves behind and upsets the beaver.

20 (CD track 10)
Performer: George Pepabano
Topic: the inlanders/deer
I'm going to sing the song of the inlanders,
The people from the east.
It's an old man singing this song;
How the Indians were having a hard time.

Their hunting was not good.
Then they saw a pack of deer coming,
Swimming across the lake towards them.
They didn't use guns to kill the deer.
They didn't use guns; they used something else

21 (CD track 11)
Performer: George Pepabano
Topic: toboggan song

These songs that I am singing, I didn't make them up,
I just sort of picked them up.
When I'm singing, I don't know about other young people,
But my grandchildren understand what I'm singing about at times.
They pick up the words; they sing along with me.
The songs that I sang, I picked up from my father
And my grandfather, generation to generation.
This is a toboggan song, how it is used for travelling.
This was the only way they travelled a long time ago.
Every type of work done or animal has its own song.
When families used to travel together parents used to sing
To put the children asleep.
This song tells a story with pictures, you could almost see them.
I learned this song from my father and taught it to my elder sons.
When we were trapping in the fall,
We sing about each way of travelling—canoe or toboggan,
About places where you are.

22
Performer: Robert Potts
Topic: the dawn

This song is about dawn. I would wake up by the dawn. I made it up by myself
a long time ago in the bush when I couldn't sleep because it was dawn. I
sang this song all the time, even when in the village. When I couldn't sleep,
I sang it in the morning. This song reminds me of the following song
[Song 23], about my sister, "dawn girl."

23
Performer: Robert Potts
Topic: the dawn girl is waking me up

I had a sister and I called her "dawn girl." The song is "The dawn girl is waking me up," as if dawn were my sister. I made the song up; it's the same as
the first song [Song 22] with words added.

24
Performer: Robert Potts
Topic: walking

When I was a young man, I would walk a long way when hunting, but I never got tired. I walked hard to find food to feed my family. I made the song up a long time ago. I look forward to going even further when hunting and sing to keep my spirits up.

(Note: Robert's wife says he used to sing it when they were in the sod houses in the bush, not when hunting. Robert sang it in the morning or afternoon.)

25
Performer: Robert Potts
Topic: bird which flies fast
The song is about a bird, "poopooson" in Cree, which flies very fast. I made the song up long ago. I sang it in the bush.

26
Performer: Robert Potts
Topic: bird which flies fast
This song has almost the same theme as the previous song, but the words are different. The poopooson is flying toward the ptarmigan, trying to catch it. It's part of somebody else's song; I heard somebody singing it. The poopooson flies after the ptarmigan, and tries to scare it.

(Note: His wife says that his mother used to sing about that, maybe that's where he got the song from.)

27
Performer: Robert Potts
Topic: geese
This is a song about geese. There were many in the bay, like a black cloud. I made it up when I was still a young man. I usually sang it when hunting and in the morning before I went out.

28 (CD track 12)
Performer: Robert Potts
Topic: low clouds
This song is about a low cloud; there is a name for every cloud. I learned it from the elders. I used to sing it at dawn; one elder used to sing it very well. This was the elder's song. I sang it because I was happy there would be another dawn again. There were times when I did kill lots of geese, just like clouds moving fast. How fast the clouds go by when its really cloudy, that's why I sing this song like this.

29 (CD track 13)
Performer: Robert Potts
Topic: fox
This song is about a fox. When I went out trapping, to check the traps, sometimes there was a fox. When I approached, the fox seemed to say, "Here's

your trap," and raised it up as if he were going to give it to me. The fox seemed to say, "Is this your trap?" I made the song up and sang it as I was approaching my traps, when there was a fox in it.

30
Performer: Robert Potts
Topic: the way the fox's tail hangs
> This is my grandfather's song. He sang it before he brought the fox into his home. I didn't catch as much fox as my grandfather. He sang about the way the fox's tail hangs.

31 (CD track 14)
Performer: Robert Potts
Topic: the beaver
> This is a song about the beaver. It dives in the winter into a hole in the ice. I used to follow the sound underneath the ice. Now he reached his point of view where he could come up. Usually when I finished blocking his way out, that's where they all were, nine in the family. The song "My Ice-chisel Is Following It" is my own. I sang it when following the beaver.

32
Performer: Robert Potts
Topic: my sister
> A very short song about my sister. The words are the same as the second song I sang, "Dawn Girl" [Song 23].

33 (CD track 15)
Performer: Robert Potts
Topic: making canoes
> The men used to sing this song about making canoes, but everyone sang it differently. It's been a long time since I sang about a canoe. I used to hear about fixing the canoe among the old men where they were standing around. That's where I heard the song about the canoe. That's when he was gathering the pieces of the canoe he was fixing.

34 (CD track 16)
Performer: Robert Potts
Topic: making canoes
> I used to hear somebody singing it. I didn't have my own song during the making of the canoe. I didn't really try to take advantage of their singing but only about the way they were making their canoes. For myself, too, I did a canoe too. But I had to find out how they were making them so that I could copy them. I was able to make a canoe, but I couldn't really start one of my own. When I was still fixing some canoes, someone used to sing the song like this: it was like gathering up some of the white fishes that get caught in fishnets.

Interpreter's comments:
He refinished a canoe.

35 (CD track 17)
Robert Potts
Topic: the canoe

I used to hear someone singing this while fixing my canoe; it's not my song. When leaving in my canoe from the shore, usually my canoe was kind of white when I finished it. As the waves bounced on the side of my canoe while speeding on, that's the way I sang it. When finishing the canoe I would paddle it in the water. I could see the fish sparkle in the sunlight under water. That's what the canoe would look like when finished.

36
Robert Potts
Topic: the loon

This song was like the loon, as the waves bounced on him when he lands on the water. That's the way I saw my canoe too, that's why I was singing like that.

37
Robert Potts
Topic: legend about the porcupine

This song is part of a legend: A man came home one evening after hunting. Only his sons were at home, his wife wasn't there. The children told him that his wife had gone off with a porcupine. They told him that a stranger had come to their home and shot a quill into the house. The porcupine said, "This is what I'll do to you if you don't come with me." The father said, "Don't leave your brother while I'm gone." He went out and followed porcupine tracks to an open space with rock. He saw porcupine quills on the ground, then stopped and sang the song: "The porcupine has arrows." This legend was told for many generations while putting the children to sleep. There is more legend: The porcupine came out and the man shot him with his arrows. The boss porcupine came out and told the hunter that he killed his son. He had told his son to look for a wife but not to bring a married woman home. "So" [said the porcupine], "he deserved what you did to him."

38 (CD track 18)
Performer: Abraham Martinhunter
Topic: the goose

This song is about the goose.
He's going to fly differently in the fall from the way he flies in the spring. This bird doesn't fool around, he means business.

Interpreter's comments:
I can't understand the words. He's talking about another bird. He calls it by another name, must be another type of Canada goose.

39
Performer: Abraham Martinhunter
Topic: the goose in spring
> I like to sing about the goose in spring.
> It's the bird that doesn't fool around.
> I like to sing about the goose,
> And when I take the white man hunting
> I sing my songs and they listen to me.
> I like to hunt the fox, but I like the goose more than anything else.
> That's all for the goose.

40 (CD track 19)
Performer: Abraham Martinhunter
Topic: the white fox
> I'm singing about the white fox.
> The two foxes are running around.
> One is very dark and one is very light.
> I was dreaming one night
> And I saw two foxes running around; one was dark and one was light.
> Then I went out to hunt in my canoe and I killed fifteen fox.
> Now I'm singing how the foxes run along the shores of the bay.
> I'm still singing about the fox.
> This time it's a white fox.
> Until I got older, that's when I began to sing
> And express my feelings through singing,
> My hunting experiences through singing.

41
Performer: Abraham Martinhunter
Topic: the otter
> This is a song about the otter.
> You know how it is when a man falls in love with a girl.
> He holds the girl.
> You know those two religious women,
> I fell in love with those two religious women.
> I dreamed that both of them were on either side of me.
> One of the other religious women couldn't come near me.
> When I awoke from my dream I had trapped two otter.
> There were supposed to be three otter, but one got away
> And couldn't come near to my traps.
> That's how I am singing about the otter.
> That's enough of the otter.

42 (CD track 20)
Performer: Abraham Martinhunter

Topic: the beaver
> Now I'm going to sing about the beaver.
> The inlanders were killing beaver.
> When they open for us to start killing beaver
> I had never seen a beaver in my life.
> The first year I started to kill beaver
> It took me one whole year to know his ways.
> I used to dream about Chipeeyoo.
> Chipeeyoo was supposed to marry this man.
> The man used to tell her to hook all the *bootsinaw* and hang them sideways.
> Bootsinaw is a part of the beaver they used for medicine; they were dried on a small stick.
> One time she didn't obey and the bootsinaw fell into the water
> When they were travelling in the winter by toboggan, moving from camp to camp. The bootsinaw had to be laid a certain way.
> She didn't listen; she could hardly wait to get to the river.
> When they got to the river, the bootsinaw fell into the river.
> "See what I told you, if you had listened to me it wouldn't have happened."
> Not too long after Chipeeyoo married the man.
> He had a brother in Rupert House.
> The brother wanted to kill him through supernatural powers.
> The man came this way, to the place called Wadash.
> You know how hard it is to get to, just along the shore here.
> They went as far as Great Whale River and that's where he died.
> So one time the brother went and checked out a beaver dam.
> He went and looked inside the dam
> And guess who was laying there, Chipeeyoo!
> Then the man said to Chipeeyoo,
> "Why didn't you tell me that I killed your man."
> He was a difficult animal to hunt, the beaver.
> One time the people were hungry; then there was a beaver.
> Somebody in Rupert House sent a beaver inland for the inlanders.
> The beaver came swimming down the river.
> This is why I don't like to see the beaver being flooded.

43

Performer: Abraham Martinhunter
Topic: the rapids around Kaniapiskau
> I loved when I saw Kaniapiskau.
> Around Kaniapiskau, there's fierce rapids there.
> My wife told me that we were being left behind.
> I was dreaming that I was paddling.
> I came to the first rapids and I saw a little bird near the rapids.
> Then my oldest son was going to take a shot at the little bird.

I told him, "Don't."
This is what I thought when they left me behind.
This is what I thought when they left me behind;
When I was paddling the rapids and the waves were huge.
I loved going through the rapids when I was in the bush.
I am going to sing differently now.

44
Performer: Abraham Martinhunter
Topic: the rapids
There was a man by the name of Gapasschicheownagon:
He had a wife by the name of Dabosoo (one who tells the truth).
He was the first man who went and checked out the Chisasibi River and its tributaries.
He and his wife travelled up through the rapids.
They had to learn how to swing their paddles.
They were using a birchbark canoe.
They came to what is now Obijoon.
Close to Obijoon are fierce rapids.
That's where Cheepayes' Back is.
The man travelled through the rapids called Cheepayes (bird).
And with the rapids there is a legend,
Because there is a rock in the centre that looks like the back of a bird.
The bird fell off the tree and into the rapids.
While he travelled he related the legend.
The bird used to sit on a tree and make these noises where the rapids were the fiercest:
Baya, baya, baya.
The bird used to sit on that limb day and night.
One day he fell off that limb and landed in the rapids
Where it was the fiercest.
He floated in the water; I don't know how he did that,
But now there's a big rock sticking out of the rapids
And we call it Cheepayesoopsawgun (Cheepayes' Back).

45 (CD track 21)
Performer: Abraham Martinhunter
Topic: the canoe and the rapids
This is my father's song about the rapids.
I'm going to sing about the canoe,
How they made them from birchbark
And sewed it up with the roots of a tree.
The women would do the sewing.
The canoe is going through the rapids.

This is about the loon, how he would be near the shore.
These were the songs that they sang as they were fixing the canoe.
Nowadays the people don't sing,
But in those days the people used to sing about everything as they were working.
I should go inland; there's so many fierce rapids
And I have seen them.

46
Performer: Abraham Martinhunter
Topic: the Inuit
In those days the Inuit were savage and fierce.
It was not easy to have an Inuit husband.
Now they behave like white men.

47 (CD track 22)
Performer: Abraham Martinhunter
Topic: on the ship
The waves were huge.
I had some whisky and I wasn't afraid of anything.
We used to be in the ship.
That old man by the name of George Spence
Used to give us some whisky.
The waves against the ship were huge.
It used to make the white man frantic.
Then we used to drink some whisky and we became brave.

48, 49, 50
Performer: Abraham Martinhunter
Topics: no explanation of songs.

51
Performer: Abraham Martinhunter
Topic: huge waves
The waves were huge.

52 (CD track 23)
Performer: Samson Lameboy
Topic: bird challenging me
Long ago the Indians knew various ways and means to survive on the land.
That's what I mainly sang about—my experiences on the land.
The people mainly sang about hunting;
The animals they hunted, the water, the rapids, the land,
While they worked, like making snowshoes.
The songs were about whatever they were doing.
Nowadays I don't think the young people do that.

They don't sing while they are out hunting or working.
The first person who taught me how to sing was my father.
We used to kill geese in the fall and in the spring.
Everytime I saw the geese I felt I could communicate with them
And they could communicate with me.
They would sing, "I don't think you can outdo me."
The geese were saying that, sort of challenging one another.
The geese would challenge him.
This song is about the bird challenging me.

Interpreter's comments:
The bird is the one speaking in this song. I can't get the words.

53 (CD track 24)
Performer: Samson Lameboy
Topic: the fish
> That's how the Indians were; they could hunt all kinds of animals.
> They could hunt under the ice for fish
> And use a spear to dig a hole in the ground
> And throw in a string or hook to the other side of the hole
> To make a net.
> That's how they feed their families on the land.
> I'm going to sing about a tool for fishing under the ice in wintertime.

Interpreter's comments:
I'm not sure what kind of tool he means. I can't get the words to this song, something about fish.

54 (CD track 25)
Performer: Samson Lameboy
Topic: woman's song: getting logs for the family
> When the hunter left, the woman would leave at the same time
> To get logs for the home, that was her job, to get firewood.
> The women, their place was in the home.
> This was one song they had; a woman made up this song.
> The woman is singing about getting logs for the family.
> That's how she cooks for the children.
> She's singing about getting firewood.
> A woman sang this song about her wood and it was passed along.

55
Performer: Samson Lameboy
Topic: white fox
> I went hunting for white fox.
> I went hunting for white fox.

56 (CD track 26)
Performer: Samson Lameboy
Topic: the sun
> It's so beautiful when the sun comes out early in the morning
> How beautiful he made it.
> How beautiful he made it.
> How beautiful he made the sky, our father
> Our father who made the sky
> How beautiful he made it.
> That's it. I don't remember where I got this song about the sun,
> Who first came out with this song.

57
Performer: Samson Lameboy
Topic: the whale
> I'm going to sing about the whale.

> *Interpreter's comments:*
> There are words, but I can't get them.

RECORDED IN 1984

58 (CD track 27)
Performer: William Jack
Topic: four poles
> This is one of my grandfather's songs. I didn't really catch the words to this song. The younger generation don't understand. It's not only me, when another old person sings I won't understand what he sings about. I'm going to sing the fish song. Remember the story with the four poles? This is my song about the four poles.

59 (CD track 28)
Performer: William Jack. Song topic: the fox
> I'm going to sing the fox song.

60 (CD track 29)
Performer: William Jack
Topic: a song to make the wind turn around which becomes a goose song
> I'm going to sing you a song made by Jimmy Redeyes.
> He had very special powers.
> He was a very powerful man, but I wasn't afraid of him; I still wrestled with him. I'm going to sing one of Jimmy's songs that he sang when he made the wind turn around.
> I'm going to sing about what Jimmy looked like
> And the song is going to go toward a goose song.

61 (CD track 30)
Performer: Samson Lameboy
Topic: woman's song: cutting wood

Long ago, men, when they were in the bush would be gone as soon as the sun came up. The same with the women: she would be out in the bush cutting wood. She cut wood because she wanted her husband to bring something home for her to cook. So women sang these kind of songs. It was mostly old women who sang the songs.

62
Performer: Samson Lameboy
Topic: the fox. Singer's comments:

Of all the game you hunt, the hardest is the fox,
Because the fox is very, very smart.
When you were hunting fox, you had to be very sly.
You couldn't even let your snowshoes brush a stick or a shrub.
You had to be very, very silent.
The fox can hear you and then you lose him,
Even when the fox is far, far away.
When there is no wind he can hear for miles when you are hunting him.
If you make a noise you will lose him.
There's different types of foxes. I'm singing about the red fox.
Some make mouse sounds, or muskrat sounds.
If you make these sounds, they'll come running to you.
The other part of the song goes: I'm tearing the paper,
I'm paying the bills with the fox as I kill.

63 (CD track 31)
Performer: Samson Lameboy
Topic: fish

When you are fishing in an area where you set your nets, sometimes you don't get fish so you have to move your nets. Fish sometimes change the area where they feed, so you have to move to another area.

64
Performer: Samson Lameboy
Topic: Hymn No. 24, Walton Hymnbook

From what I saw, from what I understand of this song,
Long ago Native people didn't think about right and wrong,
Didn't look at their actions,
Because they didn't think about it; they had to do it.
When I was growing up I knew why it was like that.
Sometimes it was some kind of punishment, if we didn't watch ourselves.
We all know that Jesus died for us on the cross.
During his lifetime Jesus too was like us.

He starved sometimes too and he was also tortured and crucified.
When he left the earth, what happened to him is happening to us too.

65
Performer: Abraham Martinhunter
Topic: getting sick on a boat

I was on the boat before I was married. I watched the boat at night. There used to be two of us on these boats, an Inuit and myself. We guided the boat because we knew the area. We came upon really bad weather when we were near the dangerous place. All the people in the boat got sick because of the waves. The song that I am singing was about them all getting sick.

66 (CD track 45)
Performer: Abraham Martinhunter
Topic: a song to sing when someone was sick

Whenever Native people came near the rough place, they were always afraid from the stories they heard. Whenever there was anybody sick they would sing the song I just sang.

67 (CD track 32)
Performer: Abraham Martinhunter
Topic: the geese

I'm going to sing about the goose and how they used to preserve the geese in wooden barrels, those first barrels. This song is about when you first start hunting in the morning; when you're sitting in the blind waiting for them to come. This is my own song.

68
Performer: Abraham Martinhunter
Topic: goose eating in water

That's another [song] while the goose is eating in the water.

69 (CD track 33)
Performer: Abraham Martinhunter
Topic: trapping fox

This is a song while I was still trapping fox. In the song I sang about the bait and also about the measuring stick. I'm singing about the white fox; I used to kill a lot. You don't see white foxes anymore, they're extinct. When he was in the water, in a canoe, he used to sing this song. This was his favourite, to be in water.

70
Performer: Abraham Martinhunter
Topic: boy singing about the water that's going to burn and the fire that's going to help him

[excerpt from myth]

So the man could hear his son singing away that night. He made two arrows. This is his [the boy's] song. He's singing about the water that's going to burn and the fire that's going to help him. He asks his father to come out. The father said, "This is not the way you're singing." The old man said, "The water's not going to boil and the canoes burn."

71 (CD track 34)
Performer: George Pepabano
Topic: beaver's plate song
> This is the beaver's plate song. We call it that because it's a trap. The beaver, that's the food—as if he's setting his plate. The song is about a beaver; I'm trying to trick them. I start from the beaver's den—all the way along to the door; it's like a bottle. You make a noise like hitting a bottle. The beaver hears that and it comes. Lots of times I caught beaver like that.
> I sang two different beaver songs.

72
Performer: George Pepabano
Topic: the beaver
> Beaver song.

73 (CD track 35)
Performer: George Pepabano
Topic: little ducks
> This song has been passed down from generation to generation. I heard it from the man who originally made it up. It's the song when they went through the rapids. It's about little ducks. You know how the falls come down and there is foaming and the little ducks are below the foaming. And you don't see them. They are just below the rapids; they don't flutter, they are just there. I'm singing about these ducks and I think the canoe is going to be the same way. If the canoe was there it would be like the little ducks.

74
Performer: George Pepabano
Topic: woman's song: the caribou
> This is one of the old ladies songs. She's dead now. She was told not to chop because she's too old. She started singing this song in the middle of the night. The old lady was singing about the caribou. You know, how they dig up their food. This was one of the happiest moments for a man [when he spots a caribou digging].

75 (CD track 36)
Performer: Mary Bearskin
Topic: making something from tendons
> This is one of my grandmother's songs. This is when she was using the tendons, when she was working with her grandmother.

76 (CD track 37)
Performer: Mary Bearskin
Topic: chopping wood

> This is when I was chopping wood. So you'll believe it now that old women sing. When there's a lot of wood near the doorway.
>
> *Husband's explanation:*
> While she was chopping wood (it was like her hunting). This was one of her favourite chores—getting wood. This is why she made a song like this. We used the wood like this, while men hunted, to cook.

77 (CD track 46)
Performers: Job and Mary Bearskin

> Hymn No. 112, Walton Hymnbook, three verses.
> Hymn No. 371, Sankey, "Look and Live."

78 (CD track 38)
Performer: Joseph Rupert
Topic: the geese

> I'm going to sing about the geese.
> When the geese come down, you hear all over where they are.
> This is my own song.
> Whenever you hear this song, you're going to think of me.
> I used to sing this song in the bush and at home too.
> This spring was early; it was hot early.
> The geese flew to their northern breeding grounds
> So the people didn't kill many.

79 (CD track 39)
Performer: Joseph Rupert
Topic: my new gun

> I'm going to sing another song.
> It's a goose song about my new gun.
> It's my new gun, so I could go hunting.

80 (CD track 40)
Performer: Joseph Rupert
Topic: man walking with snowshoes

> This song is about a man in the morning,
> When he goes out with his snowshoes.
> These make a sound when you walk.

81 (CD track 41)
Performer: Joseph Rupert
Topic: the speckled trout

> This song is about a man when he gets up early in the morning,
> As soon as the sun comes up.

I'm going to sing about a fish, when you go fishing.
A speckled trout song.

82 (CD track 42)
Performer: Joseph Rupert
Topic: the fox
   I'm singing about a fox when he is caught in his trap.
   Even when they're really far off you can see them
   Fighting the trap with his tail.

83 (CD track 43)
Performer: Joseph Rupert.
Topic: the muskrat
   This is going to be a muskrat song.

84 and 85
Performer: Joseph Rupert.
   God Save the Queen, Walton Hymnbook, No. 73, two verses
   Walton Hymnbook, No. 115, two verses

86 (CD track 44)
Performer: Alice Snowboy
Topic: Lullaby

Notes

INTRODUCTION

1 None of the northern Cree I talked to objected to my recording their songs. But such acceptance is not universal. In *Songprints: The Musical Experience of Five Shoshone Women,* Shoshone singer Angelina Wagon says, "You know, some old people, they kind of don't like to sing songs on the tape recorder. Just like my dad used to say, he said he don't care to use the tape recorder for his song. That's why I never got all of his old songs, like flag songs and the chief's song and like these old memorial songs. I never got them 'cause he didn't want to be taped.... He said it's no good to tape his songs, tape songs from people long time ago.... They always say songs hide. Any songs that do that, they don't want to be taped. Maybe that's what happened" (Vander 1988, 59).

2 Their early history is well told by Renée Fossett in her book *In Order to Live Untroubled: Inuit of the Central Arctic 1550 to 1940* (Fosset 2001).

CHAPTER ONE

1 In "Subarctic Algonquian Languages," *Handbook of North American Indians* (Helm 1981, 53), the James Bay Cree are identified by language as East Cree and Moose Cree. The Natives around Thompson, Manitoba are called, by their language, Swampy Cree, and, adjacent but further east, Woods Cree. Unless otherwise noted, all Cree words on this book are written in the East Cree dialect.

2 For the story of Roddy's life and achievements, see Bob Lowery's *The Unbeatable Breed* (Lowery 1981).

3 This bonding of couples in response to a goose call was likely based on observation of goose mating practice. Geese mate for life and stay together during all seasons. The ordering of the dance, with people leaving the dance in the same place that they entered from, may also refer to goose behaviour: like the dancers, geese return to the place of their birth each year to mate and nest. Indeed, Meyer suggests that the Cree transformed their palisade into a nest by covering it with with goose down and feathers (1990, 13).

4 Many of these Great Lakes Anishnabe moved west and now live in Manitoba, where they are also called Ojibwe and Saulteaux. In fact, in parts of northern Manitoba the Cree and Ojibwe, both Algonquian speakers, have been neighbours and relatives for about three centuries, sharing their language and culture, so much so that in Island Lake communities the Ojibwe dialect spoken is referred to as Oji-Cree.

5 "Kwashapshigan: The Conjuring Tent Ceremony." Waskaganish, 26–27 July
　 1965. Recording and transcription. In *Eastern James Bay Cree: Oral Tradition Series*,
　 Vol. 22, Part 2.

CHAPTER TWO

1 "The earliest work giving actual sea shanty verses is the *Complaynt of Scotland* of
　 1549. The form and language of these early shanties, apart from the fact that the
　 English is Chaucerian, are very much like what our sailors of the sail sang three
　 hundred years later" (Hugill 1969, 3).
2 The chronology of fur-trade events used here relies on the ethnohistory of Daniel
　 Francis and Toby Morantz, *Partners in Furs* (1983).
3 The elders were still singing canoe-making songs in the 1980s.
4 In 1841, Ojibwe Chief Peguis and twelve of his men made the long journey from
　 south of Lake Winnipeg to Norway House specifically to learn the syllabics.
5 Anne Lederman classifies Ojibwe fiddling as a syncretic music: the combina-
　 tions of two different musics to make a new one (Lederman 1987). I believe it
　 possible that Canada's northerners had a fiddle-like instrument long before sev-
　 enteenth-century contact. It may explain the receptivity of the Cree, and other
　 groups such as the Inuit, to the violin, exceptional in view of their disdain for
　 all else European. Arima and Einarsson (1976, 28), cited in Lutz 1982, page 12,
　 state that the Inuit regard the fiddle as their own stringed instrument and dis-
　 tinguish it from the western violin. Furthermore, they call their own instrument
　 a *tautirut* and the western violin a *vialak*.

CHAPTER THREE

1 The discovery of the effectiveness of this procedure, particularly with the pun-
　 gent castoreum bait from the beaver, transformed trapping in the late eighteenth
　 century and led to beaver shortages.
2 As mentioned earlier, there are also spirit plants (*atayohkanak)* that come in
　 dreams, but of eighty-six hunting songs I recorded, none are about plants.
3 In Cross Lake, Manitoba, they were called *Kih-jis-to-mah-wah-son.*

CHAPTER FOUR

1 A signal analyzer shows the difference between the two vocal timbres used. The
　 first note sung in the hymn "It Is Well" has only two harmonics, and the first
　 note of the same singer's traditional "Bird" song has six harmonics (Whidden
　 1984, 34).
2 Along with vigorous hymn-singing, the missionaries brought heavy sonorous
　 church bells into the north. What determination was required to transport these
　 immense objects into remote areas! Their sound travelled far in the relatively quiet
　 subarctic. Reverend John Thompson of Oxford House, Manitoba, recalled that
　 the tolling was slow to announce funerals, lively for weddings, and regular for
　 church services (2004).
3 Some southern evangelical gatherings which Cree and Ojibwe attend attract
　 thousands of worshippers, most of whom come to be baptized. A large tent is
　 raised, and at the beginning of the designated week a moderate drumbeat sounds,

established at one beat per second. By the end of the week, the speed increases noticeably. The preachers, many from the United States, often incorporate Indian tradition, more than did the early missionaries. They have great influence over the people, and are often the only persons who can criticize the chief.

CHAPTER FIVE

1 In the 1950s, fully twenty per cent of Canada's First Nations people were infected with this disease. Many were flown away from their families and communities to sanatoriums in the south.

CHAPTER SIX

1 That drumming has a strong affective quality is generally recognized. For example, Rodney Needham (1979) postulated that percussive sounds transmit meaningful messages about transitions in social life. Moreover, the literature connecting rhythmical drumming and psychological states is extensive. In fact, the physiological connection between the two has been confirmed, but much work remains to explain the nature of the link, work not within the scope of this book. Suffice it to say that the drums were, and remain, central to pan-Native identity.

2 The following anthropological definitions help us to understand the meaning of powwow: Leach defined ritual as "forms of symbolic statement about the social order" (1954, 14), and Turner defined it as "an epitome of the wider and spontaneous social process in which it is embodied and which ideally it controls" (1968, 273).

3 Moreover, anthropologist John Galaty suggests that "as texts, rituals are like extended metaphors that creatively use aesthetic vehicles to bring into being novel and often penetrating insights with respect to their conceptual tenors, and produce signifiers that seek out but never quite attain their signified: in this process lies the generativity of symbols" (1983, 364).

4 Anthropologist Maurice Bloch, in a paper entitled "Symbols, Song, Dance and Features of Articulation" (1974), provides insight into why music has such affective power. Briefly, his thesis is based on ritual as a communication medium. In ritual events, Bloch notes that the syntactic and linguistic freedoms of everyday communication are reduced and replaced by stylized speech and song. Bloch puts formal oratory, intoning, and finally singing in a continuum of increasing formalization. He shows that formalization drastically decreases the potential of creativity in natural language, while on the other hand it increases the authority of ritual and its potential for social control. Bloch states that the generative processes of language are normally unconscious and so complicated they are not usually raised to a conscious level. "However, when nearly all this generative potential of language (or bodily movement) has been forbidden, removed, the remaining choices left are so simple that they can suddenly be apprehended consciously" (1974, 73). Furthermore, Bloch distinguishes two kinds of meaningful language. One is the propositional force of language, the kind with which most linguists are concerned; the second is illocutionary force, also called performative force, or the language used "not to report facts but to influence people" (1964, 234). Song is characterized by illocutionary force. To quote Bloch,

"Song is therefore nothing but the end of the process of transformation from ordinary language which began with formalization" (69–70).

CHAPTER SEVEN

1 Thomas Vennum, an ethnomusicologist at the Smithsonian Institution, Washington, DC, discussed, with Maureen Matthews, the travels of the bass drum from Wisconsin to Berens River, Manitoba, in the Canadian Broadcasting Corporation radio program *Ideas* ("Fairwind's Drum," 11–12 May 1993).
2 The name "Sioux" is a French-Canadian abbreviation of "Nadowessioux," which means "small snake" or "enemy"; it was used in reference to all the different Dakota tribes such as Yankton, Teton, and Oglala.
3 The week was conducted under the auspices of the *Ma-Mow-We-Tak* Centre, a government agency that provides programs and services for Aboriginals.
4 These titles are from a CD by Young Grey Horse, called *It's Just a Tribe Thang* (CT-6297, vol. 2; Canyon Records Productions, 1999).

CONCLUSION

1 The beginning of the contact period for the northern Cree is estimated at 1682, after the English established trading posts around James and Hudson Bays in 1668 (Brownalee and Syms 1999, 49).

List of Sources

Amtmann, Willy. 1975. *Music in Canada, 1600–1800*. Cambridge, ON: Collier-Macmillan Canada.

Anderson, Robert B., and Robert M. Bone. 2003. *Natural Resources and Aboriginal People in Canada*. Concord, ON: Captus Press.

Azure, Ed. 1981. Personal Communication.

Bailey, Alfred Goldsworthy. 1969. The Conflict of European and Eastern Algonkian Cultures 1504–1700. In *A Study in Canadian Civilization*, 2nd ed. Toronto: University of Toronto Press.

Bearskin, Job. 1982 and 1984. Interview.

Bearskin, Robert. 1982. Interview.

Beaumont, Raymond M. 1990. *Discovering Norway House History.* Winnipeg: Frontier School Division No. 48.

Berkes, Fikret. 1983. *Fish and Wildlife Harvesting by the People of Chisasibi*. A report prepared for the Chisasibi Band Council. Chisasibi, Quebec.

Blacking, John. 1995. *Music, Culture and Experience*. Chicago: University of Chicago Press.

Blackned, Robert. 1984. Interview.

Blacksmith, Ken. 2002. Personal communication.

———. 2003. Interview.

Bloch, Maurice. 1974. Symbols, Song, Dance and Features of Articulation. *Archives Européennes de Sociologie* 15: 55–81.

Brightman, Robert A. 2002. *Grateful Prey.* Regina: Canadian Plains Research Center, University of Regina.

Brightnose, Jack. 1980.

Brockway, Robert. 2000. Personal communication.

Brownalee, Kevin, and Dr. E. Leigh Syms. 1999. *Kayasochi Kikawenow. Our Mother from Long Ago*. Winnipeg: Manitoba Museum of Man and Nature Aboriginal Archaeology Internship Report.

Carlisle, David B. 1975. *Contributions to Canadian Ethnology*. Ottawa: National Museums of Canada.

Chappell, Edward. 1817. *Narrative of a Voyage to Hudson Bay.* London: J. Mawman. Reprint 1970, Toronto: Coles Publishing.

Chase, Gilbert. 1966. *America's Music*. New York: McGraw-Hill.

Clarke, Neville. R., ed. 1974. *Cree-English Anglican Hymn Book.* Anglican Church of Canada, Bishop of James Bay, Diocese of Moosonee.

Coates, Ken S. 1991. *Best Left as Indians: Native–White Relations in the Yukon Territory 1840–1973.* Montreal: McGill-Queen's University Press.

Craik, Brian. 2005. Interview.

Densmore, Frances. 1910. *Chippewa Music.* New York: Da Capo Press. (Reprint, 1910. Bulletins 45 and 53, Smithsonian Institution, Bureau of American Ethnology.)

Dickason, Olive Patricia. 1992. *Canada's First Nations.* Toronto: McClelland and Stewart.

Elias, Peter Douglas. 1988. *The Dakota of the Northwest: Lessons for Survival.* Winnipeg: University of Manitoba Press.

Ellis, Henry. 1748. *A Voyage to Hudson's Bay.* London: Printed for H. Whitridge, at the Royal Exchange.

Erickson, Robert. 1975. *Sound Structure in Music.* Berkeley: University of California Press.

Fast, Vera Kathrin. 1983. The Protestant Missionary and Fur Trade Society: Initial Contact in the Hudson Bay Territory, 1820–1850. PhD dissertation, University of Manitoba, Winnipeg.

Feit, Harvey A. 1982. The Future of Hunters within Nation-States: Anthropology and the James Bay Cree. In *Politics and History in Band Societies,* ed. Eleanor Leacock and Richard Lee. Cambridge: Cambridge University Press.

———. 1983. *Shaking Tent Ceremony, Performed by Mr. Andrew Ottereyes.* Ottawa: Recording and Transcription. Report for the National Museum of Man (now the Canadian Museum of Civilization). Canadian Ethnology Service.

Flannery, Regina. 1936. "Some Aspects of James Bay Recreative Culture." *Primitive Man* 9: 49–56.

Flannery, Regina, and Ellen Smallboy. 1995. *Glimpses of a Cree Woman's Life.* Montreal and Kingston: McGill-Queen's University Press.

Fletcher, Alice C., and Francis La Flesche. 1911. *The Omaha Tribe.* Bureau of American Ethnology 27th Annual Report.

Fosset, Renée. 2001. *In Order to Live Untroubled: Inuit of the Central Arctic, 1550–1940.* Winnipeg: University of Manitoba Press.

Francis, Daniel, and Toby Morantz. 1983. *Partners in Furs: A History of the Fur Trade in Eastern James Bay 1600–1870.* Kingston and Montreal: McGill-Queen's University Press.

Fulford, George. 2002. Personal communication.

Galaty, John G. 1983. Ceremony and Society: The Poetics of Masai Ritual. *The Journal of the Royal Anthropological Institute* 18: 361–82.

Garrick, Roddy. 1981. Interviewed by Betsy Wolanski in Wabowden, MB.

Georgekish, Roderick and Bobbie. 1984. Personal communication.

Grant, Agnes. 2003. Interviewed by Lynn Whidden in Winnipeg, MB.

Grant, George. 1965. *Lament for a Nation.* Toronto: McClelland and Stewart.

Hatton, Orin T. 1986. In the Tradition: Grass Dance Musical Style and Female Pow-wow Singers. *Ethnomusicology.* Spring/Summer, 197–221.

Horden, Rev. John. Compiler. N.d. "A Collection of Psalms and Hymns in the Language of the Cree Indians of North-West America." Toronto: Anglican Book Centre.

Hotain, Mike. 1993. Interview.

Hughboy, Harry. 1982 and 1984. Interview.

Hugill, Stan. 1969. *Shanties and Sailor Songs.* New York: Praeger Publishing.

Hyman, Jacqueline. 1971. "Conflicting Perceptions of Exchange in Indian—Missionary Contact." Master's thesis, McGill University, Montreal.

Hymns Ancient and Modern. 1904. London: William Clowes and Sons.

Isham, James. 1949. *James Isham's Observations on Hudsons Bay, 1743.* Toronto: Champlain Society.

Jack, William. 1982. Interview.

Kolinski, M. 1982. "Reiteration Quotients: A Cross-Cultural Comparison." *Ethnomusicology* 26: 85–90.

Lameboy, Samson. 1982 and 1984. Interview.

Lane, Kenneth S. 1863. *The Montagnais Indians 1600–1640.* Kroeber Anthropological Society Papers, No. 7: 1–62.

Leach, E. R. 1954. *Political Systems of Highland Burma.* London: Athlone Press, University of London.

Lederman, Anne. 1987. *Old Native and Métis Fiddling in Manitoba.* Vol. 1. Toronto: Falcon Productions.

Long, John S. 1986. "The Reverend George Barnley and the James Bay Cree." *Journal of Native Studies* 6, no. 2: 313–31.

Lowery, Bob. 1981. *The Unbeatable Breed: People and Events in Northern Manitoba.* Winnipeg: Prairie Publishing.

Lutz, Maija. 1982. *Musical Traditions of the Labrador Coast Inuit.* Paper No. 79. Ottawa: National Museums of Canada.

Martinhunter, Abraham. 1982 and 1984. Interview.

Martinhunter, Daisy. 1982. Interview.

Mason, Leonard. 1967. *The Swampy Cree: A Study in Acculturation.* Paper 13. Ottawa: National Museum of Anthropology.

Meyer, David. 1990. *The Goose Dance in Swampy Cree Religion.* Paper presented at the Henry Budd 150th Anniversary Conference, The Pas, Manitoba.

Miller, J. R. *Shingwauk's Vision, A History of Native Residential Schools.* Toronto: University of Toronto Press, 1996.

Needham, Rodney. 1979. Percussion and Transition. In *Reader in Comparative Religion,* ed. William A. Lessa and Evan Z. Vogt. New York: Harper and Row.

Nettl, Bruno. 1965. Unifying Factors in Folk and Primitive Music. In *The Study of Folklore,* ed. A. Dundes. Englewood Cliffs, NJ: Prentice-Hall.

Niezen, Ronald. 1997. Healing and Conversion: Medical Evangelism in James Bay Cree Society. *Ethnohistory* 44, no. 3: 463–91.

Nute, Grace Lee. 1955. *The Voyageur.* St. Paul: Minnesota Historical Society.

Olsen, Laren. 2001. Musical Syncretism at the Missions. *Native American Studies* 15, no. 1: 13–17.

Ottereyes, Edward. 1982, 1983, and 1984. Personal communication.

Pepabano, George. 1982. Interview.

Potts, Robert. 1982. Interview.

Powers, William K. 1969. *Indians of the Southern Plains.* New York: G. P. Putnam's Sons.

Preston, Richard J. 1981. East Main Cree. In *Handbook of North American Indians. Subarctic,* vol. 6, ed. June Helm. Washington: Smithsonian Institution: 196–207.

———. 2002. *Cree Narrative. Expressing the Personal Meanings of Events.* 2nd ed. Montreal and Kingston: McGill-Queen's University Press.

Rae, John. 1882. On the Conditions and Characteristics of Some of the Native Tribes of the Hudson Bay Territories. *Society of Arts Journal* 30: 483–99.

Ross, Douglas. 2004. Personal communication.

Salisbury, Richard F. 1986. *A Homeland for the Cree. Regional Development in James Bay 1971–1981.* Kingston and Montreal: McGill-Queen's University Press.

Sankey, Ira D., compiler. 1944. *Sacred Songs and Solos with Standard Hymns, 1200 Pieces.* London: Morgan and Scott.

Seeger, Anthony. 1979. "What Can We Learn When They Sing? Vocal Genres of the Suya Indians of Central Brazil." *Ethnomusicology* 23: 373–94.

Smallboy, Ellen. 1995. *A Cree Woman's Life.* Montreal and Kingston: McGill-Queen's University Press.

Solms, Mark. 2004. "Freud Returns." *Scientific American.* May: 84–89.

Speck, Frank G. 1935. *Naskapi, The Savage Hunters of the Labrador Peninsula.* Norman: University of Oklahoma Press.

Tanner, Adrian. 1979. "Bringing Home Animals." In *Religious Ideology and Mode of Production of the Mistassini Cree Hunters.* St. John's: Institute of Social and Economic Research, Memorial University of Newfoundland.

Tedlock, Dennis. 1972. "On the Translation of Style in Oral Narrative." In *Toward New Perspectives in Folklore,* ed. Americo Paredes and Richard Bauman. Austin: University of Texas Press.

Thomas, Robert K. 1972. "Pan-Indianism." In *The American Indian Today,* ed. Stuart Levine and N. Lurie. Baltimore, MD: Penguin Books.

Thompson, John. 2004. Interview.

Turner, Steve. 2002. *Amazing Grace. The Story of America's Most Beloved Song.* New York: HarperCollins.

Turner, Victor. 1968. *The Drums of Affliction.* Oxford: Clarendon Press.

Vander, Judith. 1988. *Songprints. The Musical Experience of Five Shoshone Women.* Urbana and Chicago: University of Illinois Press.

Venne, Joe. 1988. Interview.

Visitor, Sam. 1982 and 1984. Interview.

Voyageur, Edna. 1983. Personal communication.

Whidden, Lynn. 1984. "Hymn Anomalies in Traditional Cree Song." In *Récherches Amérindiennes au Québec*. Montreal: Diffusion Parallèle 15, no. 4: 29–36.

———. 1986. *An Ethnomusicological Study of the Traditional Songs of the Chisasibi (James Bay) Cree*. PhD diss., Université de Montréal.

Wilson, Edward O. 1999. *Consilience*. New York: Vintage Books.

Wissler, Clark. 1913. *Societies and Dance Associations of the Blackfoot Indians*. Anthropological Papers of the American Museum of Natural History 11(4), 359–460.

Wolanski, Betsy. 1981. Interviewer of Roddy Garrick.

Wright, Roy. 1984. Personal communication.

Young, Egerton R. 1893. *Stories from Indian Wigwams and Northern Campfires*. London: Charles H. Kelly.

Young, Rev. George. 1897. *Manitoba Memories. Leaves from My Life in the Prairie Provinces, 1868–1884*. Toronto: William Briggs.

Bibliography

Abrahams, Roger D. 1972. "Personal Power and Social Restraint in the Definition of Folklore." In *Toward New Perspectives in Folklore*. Ed. Richard Bauman and Américo Paredes. Austin and London: University of Texas Press.

Aitchison, Jean. 1972. *General Linguistics*. London: English Universities Press.

Anderson, James Watt. 1956. *Eastern Cree Indians*. In Historic and Scientific Society of Manitoba Papers, Series III, nos. 11, 31.

Armstrong, Robert Plant. 1971. *The Affecting Presence: An Essay in Humanistic Anthropology*. Urbana: University of Illinois Press.

Asch, Michael I. 1975. "Social Context and the Musical Analysis of Slavery Drum Dance Songs." *Ethnomusicology* 19: 245–57.

Baker, Theodore. 1882. *Uber die Musik der Nordamerikanischen*. Leipzig: Druk und Verlag von Breitkopf und Hartel.

Ballantyne, Robert Michael. 1848. *Hudson Bay: On Everyday Life in the Wilds of North America*. London: Thomas Nelson and Sons.

Bateson, Gregory. 1958. *Naven*. Stanford, CA: Stanford University Press.

Bauer, George W. 1971. Cree Tales and Beliefs. *Northeast Folklore* 12: 6–70.

Bauman, Richard. 1977. *Verbal Arts as Performance*. Rowley, MA: Newbury House.

Beardy, Flora, and Robert Coutts, compilers. 1996. *Voices from Hudson Bay, Cree Stories from York Factory*. Montreal and Kingston: McGill-Queen's University Press.

Bennett, John W. 1971. A Cree Indian Reserve. In *Native Peoples*, ed. Jean Leonard Elliott. Scarborough, ON: Prentice-Hall.

Blacking, John. 1977. "Some Problems of Theory and Method in the Study of Musical Change." In *Yearbook of the International Folk Music Council* 9: 1–26.

Blok, A. 1969. "Variations in Patronage." *Sociologische Gids* 16: 365–78.

Boilès, Charles. 1977. Canto. In *Encyclopaedia*, ed. Giulio Einaudi. Torino: Einaudi.

———. 1978. *Man, Magic and Musical Occasions*. Montreal, QC: University of Montreal.

———. 1982. "A Paradigmatic Test of Articulation." In *Cross-Cultural Perspective in Musical Analysis*, ed. Timothy Rice and Robert Falck. Toronto: University of Toronto Press.

Brightman, Robert A. 1989. *Acoohkiwina and Acimowina: Traditional Narratives of the Rock Cree Indians*. Mercury Series. Ottawa: Canadian Museum of Civilization.

Brown, Jennifer S. H., and Robert Brightman. 1988. *The Orders of the Dreamed: George Nelson on Cree and Northern Ojibwa Religion and Myth, 1823.* Winnipeg: University of Manitoba Press.

Cavanaugh (Diamond), Beverley. 1982. *Music of the Netsilik Eskimo: A Study of Stability and Change.* Ottawa: National Museums of Canada.

Chance, Norman. 1968. "Conflict in Culture: Problems of Developmental Change among the Cree." *Working Papers of the Cree Developmental Change Project.* Ottawa: Canadian Research Centre for Anthropology, St. Paul University.

Childs, B. 1977. "Time and Music: A Composer's View." *Perspectives of New Music* 20: 194–219.

Cooper, John Montgomery. 1930. *Field Notes on Northern Algonkian Magic.* Twenty-third International Congress of Americanists Proceedings, 1928: 513–18.

Crawford, David. 1967. "The Jesuit Relations and Allied Documents: Early Sources for an Ethnography of Music among American Indians." *Ethnomusicology* 11: 199–206.

Cummins, Bryan D. 2002. *First Nations, First Dogs.* Calgary: Detselig Enterprises.

Darnell, Regina. 1974. "Correlates of Cree Narrative Performance." In *Explorations in the Ethnography of Speaking*, ed. R. Bauman and J. Sherzer. London: Cambridge University Press.

DeChabanon, M. 1659. *De la Musique, Considerée en elle-même et dans ses rapports avec La Parole, Les Langues, La Poésie, et Le Théâtre.* Paris: Chez Pissot, Libraire.

Degh, Linda. 1969. *Folktales and Society.* Bloomington: Indiana University Press.

Deloria, Vine. 1969. *Custer Died for Your Sins.* New York: Avon Books.

Desy, Pierette. 1973. *Fort George ou Tsesa-Sippi, Contribution à une étude sur la désintégration culturelle d'une communauté indienne de la baie James.* PhD diss., Université de Montréal, Montreal, QC.

Diamond, Beverley, M. Sam Cronk, and Franziska von Rosen. 1994. *Visions of Sound: Musical Instruments of F irst Nations Communities in Northeastern America.* Waterloo, ON: Wilfrid Laurier University Press.

Dimaggio, P., R. A. Peterson, and J. Esco. 1972. "Country Music: Ballad of the Silent Majority." In *The Sounds of Social Change*, 33–55. New York: Rand McNally.

Dissanayake, Ellen. 1988. *What Is Art For?* Seattle and London: University of Washington Press.

Elberg, N., J. K. Hyman, and Richard Salisbury. 1972. The Use of Subsistence Resources among James Bay Cree of Fort George, Paint Hills and Eastmain." In *Not by Bread Alone*, ed. J. A. Spence. Indians of Québec Association: James Bay Task Force. Mimeographed.

Ellis, Henry. 1946. "The Culture of the Northeastern Indian Hunters: A Descriptive Survey." In *Man in Northeastern North America.* Andover, MA: The Foundation.

Feit, Harvey A. 1982. "Waswanipi Realities and Adaptations: Resource Management and Cognitive Structure." PhD diss., McGill University, Montreal, QC.

Feit, Harvey A., M. E. Mackenzie, José Maillhot, and Charles Martyn. 1972. "Bibliography of Native Peoples, James Bay Region." In *Recherches Amérindiennes au Québec*. Bulletin d'Information vol. 2, spécial 1. Montreal: Societé des Récherches Amérindiennes au Québec.

Feld, Steven. 1982. "Sound and Sentiment." In *Birds, Weeping, Poetics and Song in Kaluli Expression*. Philadelphia: University of Pennsylvania.

Francis, Daniel. 1985. *A History of the Native Peoples of Québec, 1760–1867*. Ottawa: Indian and Northern Affairs Canada.

Frisbie, Charlotte J. 1980. "Vocables in Navaho Ceremonial Music." *Ethnomusicology* 24: 30.

Fulhan, Stanley A., ed. 1981. "In Search of a Future." In Manitoba Métis Federation Submission on the Migration of Native People. Winnipeg: KINEW.

Geller, Peter. 2004. *Northern Exposures. Photographing and Filming the Canadian North, 1920–45*. Vancouver: University of British Columbia Press.

Golden Bells or Hymns for Our Children. 1931. London: Children's Special Service Mission 13A, Warwick Lane, Paternoster Row, E.C.

Goody, Jack. 1961. "Religion and Ritual: The Definitional Problem." *The British Journal of Sociology* 12: 142–64.

Gould, S. 1917. *INASMUCH: Sketches of the Beginnings of the Church of England in Canada in Relation to the Indian and Eskimo Races*. Toronto: n.p.

Gould, Stephen Jay. 1987. *An Urchin in the Storm*. New York: W. W. Norton and Co.

Gourlay, K. A. 1978. "Towards a Reassessment of the Ethnomusicologist's Role in Research." *Ethnomusicology* 22: 1–35.

Hallowell, A. Irving. 1946. "Some Psychological Characteristics of the Northeastern Indians. In *Man in Northeastern North America*, ed. Frederick Johnson. Andover, MA: Phillips Academy, The Foundation.

Halpern, Ida. 1976. "Music of the Pacific Northwest Indians." *Ethnomusicology* 20: 253–71.

Hatton, Thomas. 1974. "Performance Practices of Northern Plains Pow-Wow Singing Groups." *Yearbook for Inter-American Musical Research* 10: 123–37.

———. 1986. "In the Tradition: Grass Dance Musical Style and Female Pow-wow Singers." *Ethnomusicology* (Spring/Summer): 197–221.

Helm, June, ed. 1981. "The Subarctic." In *Handbook of North American Indians*, vol. 6. Washington: Smithsonian Institution.

Herndon, Marcia. 1980. *Native American Music*. Norwood, PA: Norwood Editions.

Hind, Henry Youle. 1863. *Explorations in the Interior of the Labrador Peninsula, the Country of the Montagnais and Nasquapee Indians*. London: Longman, Roberts and Green.

Hobsbawn, Eric J. 1983. *The Invention of Tradition*. New York: Cambridge University Press.

Holden, David. 1969. "Modernization among Town and Bush Cree in Québec." *Canadian Review of Sociology and Anthropology* 64: 237–47.

Hood, Mantle. 1971. *The Ethnomusicologist*. New York: McGraw-Hill.

Horden, John D. D. (Rev.). N.d. *A Collection of Psalms and Hymns in the Language of the Cree Indians of North-West America*. Toronto, ON: Anglican Book Centre.

Howard, James H. 1983. "Pan-Indianism in Native American Music and Dance." *Ethnomusicology* 27: 71–82.

Hugill, Peter J. 1988. *The Transfer and Transformation of Ideas and Material Culture.* College Station: Texas A & M University Press.

Illich, Ivan. 1981. *Shadow Work.* London: Marion Boyars.

James Bay and Northern Quebec Native Harvesting Research Committee. 1982. *The Wealth of the Land.* Wildlife Harvests by the James Bay Cree 1972–73 to 1978–79. Quebec City, QC.

Jeans, James. 1968. *The Science of Music.* New York: Dover Publications.

Keillor, Elaine. 2005. "The Seventh Fire." CBC Radio interview for National Aboriginal Day, June 21.

Kolinski, M. 1959. "The Evaluation of Tempo: A Cross-Cultural Approach to Metro-Rhythmic Patterns." *Ethnomusicology* 17: 494–506.

———. 1965. "The Structure of Melodic Movement: A New Method of Analysis." In *Studies in Ethnomusicology*, vol 2. New York: Oak Publications.

LaPlante, Louise, and José Maillhot. 1972. Essaid'analyse d'un chant montagnais. *Recherches Amérindiennes au Québec* 11, no. 2.

LaRusic, Ignatius. 1968. "The New Auchimau: A Study of Patron–Client Relations among the Waswinipi Cree." Master's thesis, McGill University, Montreal, QC.

Leach, E. R. 1967. "Genesis as Myth." In *Myth and Cosmos*, ed. John Middleton. New York: Natural History Press.

Linton, Ralph. 1943. "Nativistic Movements." *American Anthropologist* 45: 230–40.

Lessa, William A., and Evon Z. Vogt. 1965. *Introduction to Reader in Comparative Religion.* 3rd ed. New York: Harper and Row.

Levine, Stuart. 1972. *The American Indian Today.* Ed. Stuart Levine and N. Lurie. Baltimore, MD: Penguin Books.

Levi-Strauss, Claude. 1978. *Myth and Meaning: The 1977 Massey Lectures.* Toronto: University of Toronto Press.

Lips, Julius Ernst. 1947. "Notes on Montagnais-Naskapi Economy." *Ethnos* 12: 1–78.

List, George. 1963. "The Boundaries of Speech and Song." *Ethnomusicology* 7: 1–16.

Lomax, Alan. 1968. *Folk Song Style and Culture.* New Jersey: Transaction Books.

———. 1971. "Song Structure and Social Structure." In *Readings in Ethnomusicology*, ed. David McAllester. New York: Johnson Reprint.

Lutz, Maija. 1978. *The Affects of Acculturation on Eskimo Music of Cumberland Peninsula.* Mercury Series. Ottawa: National Museum of Man.

Lytwyn, Victor P. 2002. *Muskekowuck Athinuwick. Original People of the Great Swampy Land.* Winnipeg: University of Manitoba Press.

MacKenzie, A. 1927. *The Journals and Letters of Sir Alexander MacKenzie.* Ed. W. Kaye Lamb. Cambridge: Cambridge University Press.

Malone, Bill C. 1975. *Country Music USA.* Austin: University of Texas Press.

Manitoba Indian Brotherhood. 1971. *Wahbung: Our Tomorrows.* Winnipeg, MB.

Merriam, Alan P. 1964. *The Anthropology of Music*. Evanston, IL: Northwestern University Press.

———. 1967. *Ethnomusicology of the Flathead Indians*. Chicago: Aldine.

Mitchell, Judith, ed. 1975. *Churchill River Study* (Missinipe Probe). Saskatoon, SK: Final Report 21.

Morantz, Toby. 1983. *An Ethnohistoric Study of Eastern James Bay Cree Social Organization, 1700–1850*. Mercury Series. Ottawa: National Museum of Man.

———. 1984. "Oral and Recorded History in James Bay." In *Papers of the 15th Algonquin Conference*, ed. W. Cowan. Ottawa: Carleton University.

Nadasdy, Paul. 1999. "The Politics of Traditional Ecological Knowledge: Power and the Integration of Knowledge." In *Natural Resources and Aboriginal People in Canada*, ed. Robert B. Anderson and Robert M. Bone. Concord, ON: Captus Press.

Nattiez, Jean-Jacques. 1975. *Fondements d'une sémiologie de la musique*. Paris: Union Générale d'Editions.

Nettl, Bruno. 1954. "North American Indian Music Styles." *Journal of American Folklore* 67: 45–56.

———. 1978. "Some Aspects of the History of World Music in the Twentieth Century." *Ethnomusicology* 22: 123–36.

Paine, Robert. 1971. *A Theory of Patronage and Brokerage*. Institute of Social and Economic Research, Memorial University of Newfoundland. Social and Economic Papers (2). Toronto: University of Toronto Press.

Parthun, Paul. 1979. "The Uses and Functions of Traditional Music in Ojibwa Culture." *Liberal Arts Review* 7: 69–75.

Pastor, Willi. 1912. "The Music of Primitive Peoples and Beginnings of European Music." In *Annual Report of Board of Regents of Smithsonian Institute*, 679–700. Washington DC: Smithsonian Institution.

Pelinski, Ramon. 1981. *La Musique des Inuit du Caribou*. Montreal: Presses de l'Université de Montréal.

Pember, Don. 1984. *Mass Media History*. Chicago: Science Research Associates.

Philips, Susan. 1974. "Warm Springs 'Indian Time:' How the Regulation of Participation Affects the Progression of Events." In *Explorations in the Ethnography of Speaking*, ed. R. Bauman and Joel Scherzer.

Pirzig, Robert M. 1991. *Lila*. New York: Bantam Books.

Popper, Karl. 1999. *All Life Is Problem Solving*. London: Routledge.

Powers, William. 1960. "American Indian Music." In *American Indian Hobbyist, Society of American Indian Tradition*. Alton, IL: Umphress Printing.

Preston, Richard J. 1975. "Belief in the Context of Rapid Change: An Eastern Cree Example." In *Symbols and Society*, ed. Carol E. Hill. Southern Anthropological Society.

———. 1975. *Cree Narrative: Expressing the Personal Meaning of Events*. Mercury Series, Paper 30. Ottawa: National Museum of Man, Canadian Ethnology Service.

———. 1976. *Reticence and Self-Expression: A Study of Style in Social Relationships*. In Papers of the Seventh Algonquian Conference, ed. William Cowan. Ottawa: Carleton University.

Preston, Dick, and Sarah Preston, eds. 1986. Narrated by Alice Jacob. *Cree Narrative: Let the Past Go: A Life History.* Ottawa: Paper 104, Canadian Ethnology Service.

Price, John. 1979. *Indians of Canada, Cultural Dynamics*. Scarborough, ON: Prentice-Hall.

Radin, Paul. 1956. "The Trickster." In *A Study in American Indian Mythology*. New York: Bell Publishing Company.

Rahn, Jay. 1983. *A Theory for All Music: Problems and Solutions in the Analysis of Non-Western Forms*. Toronto: University of Toronto Press.

Richardson, Boyce. 1976. *Strangers Devour the Land*. New York: Alfred A. Knopf.

Rogers, Edward S. 1967. *The Material Culture of the Mistassini*. Bulletin 2218, Anthropological Series 80. Ottawa: National Museum of Canada.

———. 1969. "Natural Environment—Social Organization Witchcraft: Cree vs. Ojibwa—A Test Case." In *Contributions to Anthropology Ecological Essays*, ed. David Damas. Bulletin 230, Anthropological Series 86. Ottawa: National Museum of Canada.

Sadie, Stanley, ed. 1980. *The New Grove Dictionary of Music and Musicians*. London: Macmillan Publishing.

Salisbury, Richard F., Fernand Filion, Farida Rawji, and Donald Stewart. 1972. *Development and James Bay: Social Implications of the Proposals for the Hydroelectric Scheme Program in the Anthropology of Development*. Montreal: McGill University.

Sapir, Edward. 1910. "Song Recitative in Paiute Mythology." *Journal of American Folklore* 23: 455–72.

———. 1921. *Language*. New York: Harcourt, Brace.

Schafer, R. Murray. 1977. *The Tuning of the World*. New York: Alfred A. Knopf.

———. 1999. *Voices of Tyranny, Temples of Silence*. Indian River, ON: Arcana Editions.

Scott, Colin H. 1983. "The Semiotics of Material Life among Wemindji Cree Hunters." PhD diss., McGill University, Montreal, QC.

Sebeok, Thomas. 1980. "Close Encounters with Canid Communication of the Third Kind." Unpublished MS.

Small, Lillian. 1972. *Indian Stories from James Bay*. Cobalt, ON: Highway Book Shop.

Smith, James G. E. "Western Woods Cree." In *Handbook of North American Indians*, ed. William C. Sturtevant. Washington DC: Smithsonian Institution.

Spicer, Edward. 1961. *Perspectives in American Indian Culture Change*. Chicago: University of Chicago Press.

Swann, Brian. 1996. *Coming to Light*. New York: Vintage Books.

Swidrovich, Cheryl. 2001. "Stanley Mission: Becoming Anglican but Remaining Cree." *Native Studies Review* 14, no. 2: 71–107.

Taylor, Garth. 1980. *Canoe Construction in a Cree Cultural Tradition*. Mercury Series, Canadian Ethnology Service, Paper 64. Ottawa: National Museum of Man.

Thompson, Stith. 1966. *Tales of the North American Indians*. Bloomington: Indiana University Press.

Thwaites, Reuben Gold, ed. 1896–1901. "The Jesuit Relations and Allied Documents." In *Travels and Explorations of the Jesuit Missionaries in New France (1610–1791)*. Cleveland: Burrows Brothers.

Toelken, Barre. 1979. *The Dynamics of Folklore*. Boston: Houghton Mifflin.

———. 1977. "The Pretty Languages of Yellowman: Genre, Mode and Texture in Navaho Coyote Narratives." In *Folklore Genres*, ed. Dan Ben-Amos. Austin: University of Texas Press.

Tulk, Esther. 2004. "Awakening to Medicine Dream." In *Canadian Folk Music Bulletin*, vol. 38. Athabasca, AB: Canadian Folk Music.

Turner, Lucien M. 1894. *Ethnology of the Ungava District*. Annual Reports of the Bureau of American Ethnology 11, 1889–1890.

Turner, Victor. 1979. "Betwixt and Between: The Liminal Period in Rites de Passage." In *Reader on Comparative Religion*, 4th ed., ed. William A. Lessa and Evon Z. Vogt. New York: Harper and Row.

———. 1982. *From Ritual to Theatre: The Human Seriousness of Play*. New York: Performing Arts Journal Publications.

Tylor, Edward B. 1979. "Animism." In *Reader in Comparative Religion*, ed. William A. Lessa and Evon Z. Vogt. New York: Harper and Row.

VanGennep, Arnold. 1972. *The Rites of Passage*. Chicago: University of Chicago Press.

Villeneuve, Larry. 1984. *The Historical Background of Indian Reserves and Settlements in the Province of Québec*. Ottawa: Research Branch, Indian and Northern Affairs Canada.

Wallace, Anthony F. C. 1972. Revitalization Movements. *American Anthropologist* 58: 264–81.

Weinstein, Martin S. 1976. Report of the Fort George Resource Use and Subsistence Economy Study. Grand Council of the Crees of Quebec, Montreal, QC.

Westfall, David, and Robert Castel. 1999. *Castel's English–Cree Dictionary and Memoirs of the Elders*. Brandon, MB: David Westfall.

Whidden, Lynn. 1983. "Cree Music and Creativity." In *Proceedings, Fourteenth Algonquin Conference*, ed. William Cowan. Ottawa: Carleton University.

———. 1983. "Ritual Powwow Music: Its Power and Poetics." *Canadian Folk Music Journal* 11: 3–11. Calgary: Canadian Folk Music Society.

———. 1984. "How Can You Dance to Beethoven?: Native People and Country Music." *Canadian University Music Review* 5: 83–107. Toronto: Becker Associates.

———. 1989. "The Cree Soundworld as Described by George Nelson, 1823." Proceedings of the First Conference on Ethnomusicology in Canada. Toronto: Institute for Canadian Music.

———. 1989. "Cree Hymnody as Traditional Song." In *The Hymn* (July). Fort Worth, TX: Hymn Society of America.

———. 1990. Powwow Singers. Article update for *Encyclopaedia of Music in Canada*. Toronto: University of Toronto Press.

———. 1992. "Global Restructuring: Is the Powwow Becoming a World Music? In *Canadian Issues*, vol. 14. Montreal: Association for Canadian Studies.

———. 1994. "An Essay on Maps both Mental and Physical." *Tuning of the World Conference Documents. International Conference for Acoustic Ecology*, 1993.

———. 1996. "Review Essay: Published Sound Recordings of North American Native Music." *Journal of American Folklore* (Spring).

———. 1998. "Rethinking Native Music Scholarship." *Canadian Journal of Native Studies* 18, no. 1.

———. 2000. "Métis Music." In *A Métis Historiography and Annotated Bibliography*. Louis Riel Institute/Gabriel Dumont Institute Millennium Project. Winnipeg: Pemmican Publications.

———. 2001. "Putting the Indian into Cowboy Music." In Canadian Folk Music Bulletin 35, no. 1 (May). Athabasca, AB: Canadian Folk Music.

———. 2001. "A Few Wrong Notes Don't Matter." *Ostinato* 27, no. 2 (Winter). St. Lambert, QC: Carl Orff, Canada.

———. 2003. "Songs Their Fathers Sang." *Ethnologies* 25, no. 2. Quebec City: Université de Laval.

———. 2003. "Gnaah and the Trout Song." *Proceedings of Eighth Workshop on the Structure and Constituency of Languages of America* (WSCLA). Vancouver: University of British Columbia, Department of Linguisitics.

Wilson, Edward O. 1984. *Biophilia*. Cambridge, MA: Harvard University Press.

Witmer, Robert. 1973. "Recent Change in the Musical Culture of the Blood Indians of Alberta, Canada." *Yearbook for Inter-American Musical Research* 9: 64–94.

Wittenborn, R., and C. Biegert. 1981. *James Bay Project: A River Drowned by Water*. Montreal: Montreal Museum of Fine Art.

Yeston, Maury. 1976. *The Stratification of Musical Rhythm*. New Haven and London: Yale University Press.

Index

Essential Song
Three Decades of Northern Cree Music

Track List
Track Number, Artist, Song Topic, Collection Number (App. II), Song Length
Tracks 1–46 recorded in Quebec, tracks 47–52 in Manitoba.

Listen at: https://www.wlupress.wlu.ca/Books/E/Essential-Song

1 William Jack – Fox (2) 1:18
2 William Jack – Beaver (3) 0:57
3 William Jack – Lake Trout (4) 0:33
4 William Jack – Rabbit (5) 1:18
5 William Jack – Seagull (6) 0:40
6 William Jack – Winterbird (7) 1:14
7 George Pepabano – Partridge (13) 0:58
8 George Pepabano – Man & Bear (14) 0:44
9 George Pepabano – Canoe (18) 0:50
10 George Pepabano – The Inlanders (20) 1:00
11 George Pepabano – Toboggan (21) 1:04
12 Robert Potts – Low Clouds (28) 0:44
13 Robert Potts – Fox (29) 0:38
14 Robert Potts – Beaver (31) 0:24
15 Robert Potts – Making Canoes (33) 0:21
16 Robert Potts – Canoes (34) 0:11
17 Robert Potts – Canoe (35) 0:06
18 Abraham Martinhunter – Goose (38) 4:19
19 Abraham Martinhunter – White Fox (40) 2:29
20 Abraham Martinhunter – Beaver (42) 2:47
21 Abraham Martinhunter – Canoe & Rapids (45) 1:44
22 Abraham Martinhunter – The Waves Were Huge (47) 0:10
23 Samson Lameboy – The Geese Challenging Me (52) 0:54
24 Samson Lameboy – Fish (53) 1:06
25 Samson Lameboy – Woman Getting Firewood (54) 0:53
26 Samson Lameboy – The Sun in the Morning (56) 0:28
27 William Jack – Four Poles (58) 0:39
28 William Jack – Fox (59) 1:18
29 William Jack – Song That Made the Wind Turn Around (60) 1:29
30 Samson Lameboy – Woman's Song for Cutting Wood (61) 1:48
31 Samson Lameboy – Fishing (63) 0:13
32 Abraham Martinhunter – How They Preserved Geese in Wooden Barrels (67) 0:36
33 Abraham Martinhunter – Trapping Fox (69) 1:40
34 George Pepabano – Beaver's Plate (71) 0:48
35 George Pepabano – The Little Ducks and the Rapids (73) 0:31
36 Mary Bearskin – Working with the Tendons (75) 0:35
37 Mary Bearskin – Chopping Wood (76)1:16
38 Joseph Rupert – The Geese Flew to Their Northern Breeding Grounds (78)1:14
39 Joseph Rupert – Goose Song about My New Gun (79) 0:47
40 Joseph Rupert – A Man in the Morning with His Snowshoes (80) 1:40
41 Joseph Rupert – A Speckled Trout Song (81) 0:37
42 Joseph Rupert – Fox When He Is Caught in His Trap (82) 0:54
43 Joseph Rupert – Muskrat (83) 1:24
44 Alice Snowboy – Lullaby (86) 2:53
45 Abraham Martinhunter – The Great Physician (66) 0:27
46 Joseph and Mary Bearskin – Hymn, Look and Live (77) 4:24
47 Jack Brightnose – Charlie Campbell 2:36
48 Jack Brightnose – Trapline Blues 3:09
49 Robert Castel – Jesus ota nit-oyan 2:28
50 Robert Castel – Amazing Grace 3:17
51 Ed Azure – Red Sky Song 1:04
52 Ed Azure – 49er 1:34

Books in the Indigenous Studies Series
Published by Wilfrid Laurier University Press

Blockades and Resistance: Studies in Actions of Peace and the Temagami Blockades of 1988–89 | Bruce W. Hodgins, Ute Lischke, and David T. McNab, editors | 2003 | 0-88920-381-4

Walking a Tightrope: Aboriginal People and Their Representations | Ute Lischke and David T. McNab, editors | 2005 | 978-0-88920-484-3

Indian Country: Essays on Contemporary Native Culture | Gail Guthrie Valaskakis | 2005 | photos | 978-0-88920-479-9

Words of the Huron | John L. Steckley | 2007 | 978-0-88920-516-1

Essential Song: Three Decades of Northern Cree Music | Lynn Whidden | 2007 | 978-0-88920-459-1

The Long Journey of a Forgotten People: Métis Identities and Family Histories | Ute Lischke and David T. McNab, editors | 2007 | 978-0-88920-523-9

From the Iron House: Imprisonment in First Nations Writing | Deena Rymhs | 2008: 978-1-55458-021-7 hardcover | 2016: 978-1-55458-580-9 paper

Lines Drawn upon the Water: First Nations and the Great Lakes Borders and Borderlands | Karl S. Hele, editor | 2008: 978-1-55458-004-0 hardcover | 2016: 978-1-55458-487-1 paper

Troubling Tricksters: Revisioning Critical Conversations | Linda M. Morra and Deanna Reder, editors | 2009 | 978-1-55458-181-8

Aboriginal Peoples in Canadian Cities: Transformations and Continuities | Heather A. Howard and Craig Proulx, editors | 2011 | 978-1-055458-260-0

Bridging Two Peoples: Chief Peter E. Jones, 1843–1909 | Allan Sherwin | 2012 | 978-1-55458-633-2

The Nature of Empires and the Empires of Nature: Indigenous Peoples and the Great Lakes Environment | Karl S. Hele, editor | 2013: 978-1-55458-328-7 | 2016: 978-1-55458-488-8 paper

The Eighteenth-Century Wyandot: A Clan-Based Study | John L. Steckley | 2014 | 978-1-55458-956-2

Indigenous Poetics in Canada | Neal McLeod, editor | 2014 | 978-1-55458-982-1

Literary Land Claims: The "Indian Land Question" from Pontiac's War to Attawapiskat | Margery Fee | 2015 | 978-1-77112-119-4

Learn, Teach, Challenge: Approaching Indigenous Literatures | Deanna Reder and Linda M. Morra, editors | 2016 | 978-1-77112-185-9

Arts of Engagement: Taking Aesthetic Action In and Beyond the Truth and Reconciliation Commission of Canada | Dylan Robinson and Keavy Martin, editors | 2016 | 978-1-77112-169-9

Why Indigenous Literatures Matter | Daniel Heath Justice | 2017 | 978-1-77112-176-7

Read, Listen, Tell: Indigenous Stories from Turtle Island | Sophie McCall, David Gaertner, Gabrielle L'Hirondelle Hill, and Deanna Reder, editors | 2017 | 978-1-77112-300-6

Violence Against Indigenous Women: Literature, Activism, Resistance | Allison Hargreaves | 2017 | 978-1-77112-239-9

Activating the Heart: Storytelling, Knowledge Sharing, and Relationship | Julia Christensen, Lisa Szabo-Jones, and Christopher Cox, editors | 2017 | 978-1-77112-219-1

The Homing Place: Indigenous and Settler Literary Legacies of the Atlantic | Rachel Bryant | 2017 | 978-1-77112-286-3

www.ingramcontent.com/pod-product-compliance
Lightning Source LLC
Chambersburg PA
CBHW070930030426
42336CB00014BA/2606